Cheryl, Thank

NO MORE LEMONS

A Testimony of Faith, Deliverance, &
The Unmatched Power of God

LATOSHA CARTER

ISBN-13: 978-0692069813
ISBN-10: 069206981X

Printed in the United States of America

This book is dedicated to the One who is able to do far more abundantly than I can ask or even imagine...and to those who believe He's also able to do the same for them.

Contents

Acknowledgments

First and foremost, I would like to give honor and reverence to my Lord and Savior Jesus Christ, who is and will forever be the keeper of my soul. I thank You for having me in mind before I was created and for setting me apart. In the process of writing this book, You have allowed me to experience healing, deliverance, revelation, restoration, and You have ultimately redeemed me. Thank You for the vision and provision. You gave me the idea of this book in a time I needed it most, for this I am exceedingly grateful. I am nothing without You, this book would be nothing without You, nor could I have done this without the faith and confidence I have in You. I love You my Heavenly Father!

To my BFF, my right-hand man, my "Homie Lover Friend," my husband. What can I say, God has brought us a mighty long way. You are one of the main reasons behind this smile! I am extremely proud of the man you have become, and I am honored to call you my husband. Thank you for believing in me and encouraging me in times I wanted to give up. Thank you for your unwavering support and love you pour into my life. I can't imagine experiencing life's journey with anyone else and having you by my side makes it all worth it. I appreciate your selflessness and you believing in the vision of this book. All the good that comes from it, I am looking forward to sharing with you. I praise God for you. Love you always and forever!

To my daughter, Savannah Christian Carter: you are my greatest accomplishment! You welcomed me into motherhood with open arms and I am so very grateful for you. You have given my life purpose, joy and have brought an entire new meaning to the word love. I prayed for a little girl. Not only did God answer my prayers, He blessed me beyond what I could have ever imagined. The hard work that went into making this book a reality is all because of you. You have given me something to work for, something to fight for, and have allowed me to discover strength I hadn't realize I possessed. A better life for you than I had is all I desire. I hope to make you as proud to have me as your mother, just as I am to have you as my daughter. My little angel, mommy loves you more than you will ever know.

To my Shero, my mother Sandra Blaylock: without you there's no me. As I reflect on the sacrifices and unconditional love you have given me my entire life, I am overwhelmed with gratefulness. I know what love is because of the love you've shown and instilled in me. You are a woman with a heart of gold, who always manages to see the good in people, which happens to be one of the characteristics I love most about you. I immensely appreciate the steadfast support you have given me and continue to give me. Thank you for always being by my side, believing in me and cheering me on; for this I am eternally grateful. I hope I am blessed to be as great of a mother to Savannah as you are and have always been to me. If there was a book on the way mothers should love their children, you would be the author. I love you Mama.

To my daddy, Robert Blaylock: without you there's no me. I am grateful for the relationship we now have, and I thank God for opening my heart to receive and understand life is not always going to be the way we envision it, but with hope, forgiveness and understanding, anything is possible. I'm glad that God has established our relationship to its rightful place while also allowing me to see you the way He expects me to. I want you to know that I love you with all my heart, and it will forever outweigh anything from the past.

I would like to express my gratitude to those who saw me through the process of this book. My covering, Pastor Dressel Huston and Lady Lydia Huston of Open Door Christian Center, Caryn Lewis, Teela Davis, Jennifer Mister, Stephanie Rhodes, Lerin Wagner, Lisa Mitchell, Kendahle Artist, Dawn Ambus, Anaesha Whitaker, Koran Bolden, my brother Brandon Blaylock, my cousin Kenneth Johnson and my aunt Eva Johnson. Whether you prayed, supported, encouraged, proofread, gave feedback, shared ideas or have simply shown excitement for this book, I truly appreciate you!

I would also like to thank Angie Renee' of Nuance Publishing and Lance Thurman of Lance Omar Thurman Photography.

Last but not least: I would like to thank my family and friends who have loved and supported me over the course of the years. I've learned that it's not what we have in life, but who we have in our life that matters. I want you all to know the role each of you have played in my life has been vital in me becoming the woman I am today.

I thank you and love you all!

Foreword

What do you do when you've reached the end of your rope, when you've run out of gas, or when you've exhausted all your past options? This book is a testimony of a woman who has faced countless trials, both spiritually and emotionally; yet the fighter within her, along with her faith in God, gave her cause to not give up. Although she struggled with completely trusting God, this book reveals the processes she underwent to get there and what trusting Him can do. My wife is a strong woman of God and for the past several years, her faith and will to please the Lord has greatly been tested. Her testimony reflects how prayer, putting God first, and staying faithful to His word, will bring you out of the enemy's line of fire. I compare Tosha's story to David and Goliath, because she has overcome giants that no one ever expected her to. Throughout her journey, God allowed her to encounter certain life changing events, trials, tribulations, battles and tests, as a way for her to completely surrender to Him. Although she always had a heart for God, He desired more from her. Like the potter's wheel, God's desire to mold her into His masterpiece totally outweighed any plans she or the enemy had for her life. What I admire most about my wife is that she's a fighter; she's fearless and an altogether conqueror. She is not a victim of her circumstances; she's the epitome of strength. She did not allow her struggles to define her negatively. Instead, they have shaped her into the phenomenal woman she is today.

Like Paul, "the Apostle of Grace", I have received redemption in Christ Jesus and because of God's saving power, I stand today a different man than I was back then. Like many of us, there have been times we have done things we haven't been too proud of. My mistakes have caused my wife a great deal of pain, my marriage turmoil, but most importantly they have hurt God. Gratefully, through God I have received a true deliverance and proud of the man I am today. However, to gain the full measure of the man I have become, it's necessary to take a look at the man I once was. I am excited to declare my life has since then been changed as I am now living a life for Christ and the advancement of His kingdom.

With this being said, I invite you to witness how the power of God is manifested throughout this dynamic story.

Chris Carter

Preface

God is truly in the business of shaping and molding us into what He purposes us to be. Although it doesn't always look good nor feel good, it is necessary. I realized everything I experienced was all a part of God's perfect plan for my life. What I've always liked about myself is my willingness and capability of transparency. I truly believe we can heal as we reveal. So many people are concerned with perception when inside they're hurting. While being worried with what people are going to say and think, they keep it to themselves instead of releasing it, and ultimately; they suffer. Everything we go through in life has a purpose. Our experiences, both good and bad, are not always meant to be kept a secret. Sometimes our experiences are meant to be shared to help someone else who is hurting. I recall listening to one of my favorite Gospel entertainers in an interview. He stated, "I can impress you with all my accolades and accomplishments, but I can change you by telling you about my struggles." I connected to this statement so much. It gave me the courage to be settled in my spirit regarding sharing my testimony. It's more important for me to win souls than it is to win popularity. In this testimony of my life, I truly bare it all. What I believe to be so awesome is while experiencing the most difficult time in my life, God gave me the strength to write about it. For this reason, there are moments within this book that consist of raw emotions. I could have chosen to rewrite my feelings making it appear to be pretty and perfect. However, I am a believer that people relate to real. I am confident that sharing my story is going to help someone who has encountered the same level of pain and some of the same experiences as I did. I am here to let you know that you are not alone. I embrace where I've been and am most excited about where I am going. My trials and past mistakes do not define who I am, but they have simply helped to push me toward my true purpose in Christ. I hope my testimony encourages, inspires, and gives someone courage to never give up.

CHAPTER ONE

In The Beginning

And we know that God causes everything to work together for the good of those who love God and are called according to his purpose for them.

~Romans 8:28~

We've all heard the saying, "When life gives you lemons, make lemonade." What do you do when you're unable to make lemonade? All too many times I've found myself in this predicament, but never to this extreme. How did I get here? This is the question I've asked myself time and time again. For that question to be answered, I realized I had to revisit my childhood.

Born in St. Louis, Missouri in the year of 1981, I was the firstborn of a young, 19-year-old woman from Wellston and a young, 21-year-old man from Pagedale. My mother relocated to Memphis, Tennessee with her parents and during a visit back to St. Louis, she met my father. Handsome, a nice dresser, and a great sense of humor is what my mother described him as. They met and immediately fell in love. A few years later, I was born; and almost two years later, my first born brother was born. My father was a ladies' man. So much of a ladies' man that he had his third child outside of the relationship he had with my mother. My mother, along with insecurities she inherited from her childhood, continued to give him chance after chance. What I admire about my mother is that she treated my brother just as he was her child. This was strength. My mother is, and has always been, a woman of integrity with a heart of gold. She could have chosen to be bitter, angry, and resentful regarding the situation. However, she chose love. For this reason and many more she is forever labeled phenomenal in my eyes.

During my parent's relationship, abuse began to take place. My father was both physically and verbally abusive, mainly when he would drink. My mother chose to stay with him in hopes he would eventually change. As women, we want badly to believe in the man we love; even if it means putting ourselves second and making them priority, even if it means settling, and even if it means not receiving the respect we very well deserve. My mother sacrificed her happiness for someone who didn't appreciate her. She longed for what every woman wants, a happily ever after, and stayed in hopes she would eventually get it. Later down the line, she gave birth to my baby brother. My mother ultimately wanted to keep her family together. With limited education, diagnosed with dyslexia as a child, along with three children to care for, she struggled. However, it didn't stop her; she was a survivor. She sacrificed so much and did whatever it took to provide for my brothers and me. From upholstering furniture, to doing hair, and babysitting kids; she made sure bills were paid and food was on the table. She was determined not to give up. The first time I learned about faith was from my mother. No matter how tough times got, she never lost her faith. Aside from the dysfunction in our household, my mother made it her priority to instill good values and morals into her children. The positive always overpowered the negative. Although she had very little, what she implanted within her children was grand.

When I was eleven years old, my parents got married. I remember the wedding day as if it was just yesterday. The sun was shining, but my spirit was dim. I had seen just about everything my father had put my mother through; the disrespectful way he spoke to her, the way he treated her, the abuse, and even the way he spoke to my brother and I. My baby brother hadn't experienced much of the things we had. I had seen it all and the last thing I wanted was for my parents to get married. As time went on, nothing really changed except for my behavior. I began to develop a strong resentment toward my father. I had zero respect for him and it showed. I always had a mouth on me, as my mother would say. I didn't have a problem standing up to my father for the way he would treat my mother. As crazy as it may sound, it appeared that my father had more respect for me than he did my mother. I took on the role of being my mother's protector. When my father would disrespect her, I would come to her defense. As a young child, I made the decision not to allow a man to treat me the way my father treated my mother. I wanted better and would deserve better just as my mother had. We don't always recognize our worth, and this is part of the reason my mother stayed with my father. Poor self-esteem accompanied by insecurities will have us tolerating behaviors we shouldn't and staying in relationships we know aren't what God intended for us. I gained strength through what my mother endured. It caused me to become resilient, fearless, and a woman who stood up for herself and for what's right even if it meant standing alone.

CHAPTER TWO

Facing The Facts

And you will know the truth, and the truth will set you free.

~John 8:32~

I recall as a small child being "daddy's little girl," but as I got a little older I began to form my own opinion of him based off the things I saw. What I admired about my mother is, aside from how my father treated her, she taught us to respect him. However, it was challenging for me to respect someone who was causing our family so much pain. I hated the negative impact alcohol had on my father. Sometimes he would be this fun and humorous man and other times he was angry and argumentative. Living on pins and needles, not knowing what type of mood my father would be in was common in our home. On the other hand, our home was the place to be. My mother was known as "Aunt San" to pretty much everyone in the neighborhood. There was always a house full of people; family and friends who would come over just to hang out. Aside from all the people, parties, family gatherings, etc., not too many people knew what we were dealing with once the music stopped, once the crowd disappeared, and once it was just us. My mother did a good job in hiding her pain and putting on a good face. She kept a smile on her face and was devoted to making everyone around her happy even though she was hurting inside. Although I was her daughter and a child, I was her comfort. I was wise and mature beyond my years, mainly because of the level of responsibility that was placed on me as a child. At the time, I didn't pay much attention to it. I welcomed it with no complaints, I felt I was strong enough to handle it. I've always been extremely close to my mother and I would do anything to protect her. The resentment toward my father was known, but what I didn't know was all those years of protecting and defending my mother, would result in me eventually resenting her.

When I was younger, we were actively involved in church. My father never attended church with us. Back then I didn't really give it much thought, but as an adult I see how it set the foundation for our family. As a child, church was something I was made to do and not something I necessarily wanted to do. When I got a little older, we stopped attending. It wasn't until I became an adult that I began to establish a personal relationship with God. During this time, my view of everything that occurred in my childhood began to change. God revealed to me quickly that although my father hadn't been the father I needed, it was still my responsibility to honor him. From this point, I began to work toward forgiving my father. What I discovered is that forgiving him wasn't as challenging as I expected it to be.

After thirty plus years of my parents being together, my mother made the decision to divorce my father. It had been several years since the physical abuse ended, yet the verbal abuse continued. However, there was a change; something was different. My mother wasn't this timid woman she had been for so long; she began standing up for herself. It was as if she suddenly found her voice. This was the starting point of a new life for her. Shortly after their divorce, she began spending her time as a motivational speaker. She felt it was important for her to share her story in an effort of preventing others from going through the same things she endured. I remember her first speaking engagement; I was excited and proud of her. I admired her strength and the courage she possessed in sharing such intimate parts of her life with a group of strangers. During one of her speaking engagements, she asked me to open the event with prayer. Before I began praying, I quoted statistics about domestic abuse and I then did something that wasn't on my agenda. I began sharing my outlook on what my mother had gone through. Before I realized it, I shared with everyone, including my mother, that I resented her. Shocked that I had chosen to reveal this in that moment, I could see the look of hurt and guilt on my mother's face. However, it was too late, the words had already come out my mouth. As much as this moment was about my mother, I realized it had a lot to do with me as well. For many years, I never knew those feelings even existed. I was so focused on being there for my mother and protecting her that I ignored my own feelings. It's as if I was numb all those years. The moment I tapped into my truth, I recognized that I blamed my mother for staying with my father and allowing us to be raised in dysfunction. This was the true starting point of my healing process. As I listened to her story, I received revelation. Things I had never known were revealed, questions I always wanted answered, were answered. I began to see my mother in a different light; I understood why she stayed for so long. A weight was lifted on that day, I believe for both me and my mother. It's amazing that what we believe to be the worst circumstance of our life can turn out to be a blessing. Not only did I begin to understand my mother better, I began to understand myself as well.

CHAPTER THREE

Every Girl Needs Her Father

And this same God who takes care of me will supply
all your needs from his glorious riches, which have
been given to us in Christ Jesus.

~Philippians 4:19~

Because I was the only girl among my siblings, I spent a lot of time at my aunt's house with my girl cousins. The relationship they had with their father was a reminder of what I didn't have with mine. I enjoyed being around them, because it helped to fill the void in my life. However, it brought on a considerable amount of sadness. I eventually ignored these feelings and went on with life, not knowing that I would have to face the facts someday.

My mother instilled in her children early on the importance of education. Having dealt with her own struggles educationally, she wanted more for us. I always felt she expected more of me than she did my siblings; she was harder on me for some reason. She made it very clear that receiving a higher education was my only option. Therefore, after graduating high school I enrolled at Southern Illinois University Edwardsville. During my time in college, I began to see things through a different lens. My perspective broadened. I met different people from different backgrounds. Not only was my college experience instrumental in me becoming the person I am today, it was also during this time that I began to pay close attention to an area in my life that I tried to hide and forget; a healthy relationship with my father. Two of my friends were very close with their fathers and they spoke highly of them. All those years, I thought I was okay and I had grown to accept things for what they were; then suddenly I began to realize the truth. I wasn't okay. I longed for that same type of relationship my friends spoke of having with their fathers.

Although my father physically lived in the home, he wasn't there for me the way I needed him to be. He didn't teach me those things a father teaches their daughter, things she'll later need in life. Don't get me wrong, my father was not a horrible person. He had a good heart, but he also made some mistakes. I eventually realized he just didn't know exactly what fatherhood truly consisted of. There are two types of people; there are those who choose to learn from their experiences and then there are those who don't. It took me some time to get it, but I understand that I lacked because my father also lacked.

To lack means to be without or to not have enough of something. Whether its finances, relationships, etc., we all know how it feels to be without. What I have learned is that whatever area in which you're lacking, it is the same area in which God plans to provide in. God sometimes allows us to be without something as a way for us to realize how much we need Him. As I matured spiritually, things became clear. Growing up, I have always had more male friends than female friends. When I was younger, I thought it was because of the type of personality I had and that I meshed well with guys. I was that girl who would be with a group of guys playing football, riding bikes, climbing trees, playing in creeks, and jumping neighborhood fences. I was always told I was cool and down to earth. I was comfortable being the only girl in a group of guys. In fact, my childhood best friend is a guy. What I eventually realized, is that the real reason I connected more with the opposite sex was because of the lack of relationship I had with my father. Subconsciously, I looked to my homeboys to somehow fill that void. Loyalty and those close to me having my back was extremely important. The issue wasn't that my father wouldn't have stood up for me and protected me if I needed him to, but, it was difficult for me to view him as being that person considering his behavior toward my mother. Therefore, I began to place that expectation on other males in my life.

The first man a girl loves is her father, and the first example she receives of how a woman should be treated is from her father. Now if this example is nonexistent or unhealthy, it may cause that little girl who will one day become a woman to face relationship challenges with other men. Some women may struggle with feelings of low self-esteem and unworthiness. Women who lack in this area, may seek to fill this void in other ways such as settling and allowing others to define them. Although this has never been the case for me, I did in fact struggle with some things. What most people don't know, is that I struggled with depression. Everyone has always viewed me as being a strong person. Although this is true, it's also true that strong people also have their struggles. In hindsight, my childhood experiences impacted me tremendously. Not realizing it until I had gotten older, but the void in my relationship with my father caused me to be in search of loyalty and protection from the opposite sex. I had been placing unrealistic expectations on certain people. For example, I placed such a great expectation on my brother. Primarily because we had experienced most of the same things as children, and I expected for him to understand. What I failed to realize, was that he was incapable of being what I needed, because he too hadn't received what he needed from our father. The expectations I set for the males in my life, including my brothers, uncles, cousins, homeboys, boyfriends, and eventually my husband, were relative to what I lacked in my relationship with my father. I was searching for a father figure within those relationships, but the reality is that it's impossible for a brother or husband to fulfill a father's role to their sister or wife. Only my father could achieve this. Everyone has their specific role and position in a person's life. My father's role was simply that, to be my father. Although he didn't fulfill his role in the way I felt he should have, it was no one else's responsibility to do so.

As I got closer to God, my perception of my father changed. I understood him better and understood why he made the mistakes he did. Alcoholism is an addiction and it consumed him. I realized that for me to move forward with my life I had to forgive my father. I no longer wanted to live in bondage. I wanted God to heal my heart from all the pain attached to my childhood. As I began to reflect over my life, I realized God's ability of restoration is amazing. All is forgiven; the resentment, pain, and anger are gone. My experiences are no longer viewed as negative memories I tried so hard to forget, but have now become a consumption of remembrances that have formed me into the woman I am today. I've learned there is nothing too big for God. I never thought my feelings toward my father would change. My plan all along was when I became an adult, I wasn't going to have any dealings with him, but God surely showed me who's in control.

In life, we think we have it all figured out, we think we know what's best for our lives. Truth is, God is the author and finisher of our fate. He created us and therefore He knows exactly what we need and when we need it. He had a plan for my life; He repaired a broken relationship between a father and a daughter. A few years ago, my father and I had a conversation. In that conversation, he acknowledged the mistakes he made and not being the father his children deserved. Even though I grew up with so much anger towards my father, the unconditional love outweighed it all. Because of it, I have been able to forgive and let go of the past and have begun to accept him for who he is; flaws and all. The point here is that no one is perfect. Although I needed more from my father, he was only able to give me what he was capable of. As an adult, but also being a woman of God, I now get it. Our past has a profound way of shaping us into who we will become, but it doesn't have to negatively dictate our future. Through God's Grace and Mercy, there's always hope for a new beginning.

The silver lining is that we sometimes don't understand there's purpose in our lacking. What we sometimes lack is all a part of God's plan to provide. God allows us to lack, because He wants us to fully lean and depend on Him. I praise Him for what I didn't have back then, because it has allowed me to appreciate what I do have now. I have experienced God's ability of completely supplying all my needs. So often, we run to man for the answers; when all along God holds the key. He helped me to realize and understand I didn't need to look to man as a substitute. He was all I needed then and still all I need today.

CHAPTER FOUR

Superwoman

She is clothed in strength and dignity; and she laughs without fear of the future.

~Proverbs 31:25~

What is it that makes a woman strong? Some people associate strength with physical ability. However, that's not always the case. I believe it's a woman's struggles, sacrifices, selflessness, and forgiveness that truly makes her strong. A woman of strength has endured pain and heart wrenching experiences, yet never allowed it to overtake her. She's been through hell and high-water, yet she's managed to come out on top and better than before. This type of woman is self-sufficient, powerful, loving, fearless, and remains true to who she is. She carries the weight of the world on her shoulders, and makes it look so easy. The world is full of strong women with many different experiences, and although these experiences may not always be good, they are vital in shaping and molding us into the strong women we are.

Early on, I developed a persona of being tough; but later I realized it was only a defense mechanism because of what I had experienced throughout my childhood. Although I was strong, I wasn't as hard or as tough as I may have wanted to appear. I was sensitive, compassionate and loving; yet I chose to keep the softer side of me hidden. I was guarded, because I did not want anyone to hurt me, especially a man. I witnessed all the hell my father put my mother through; the sadness and depression that consumed her and I wasn't going to tolerate a man treating me that way. My childhood consisted of an array of memories, both good and bad. Although life is comprised of many memories, there are those that stick out more than others. I'll never forget the time I was in the third grade. I entered the "I Love My Mom Because" contest and won. In my essay, I revealed my mother's struggle with dyslexia and how I would help her to read. After I won, and my peers found out, they talked about me. As hurtful as it was, I stood strong. Even though I regretted ever sharing something so private, I didn't allow it to get the best of me. For many years after, I kept it a secret. It wasn't until later in life that I decided to no longer allow myself to be ashamed of it. No one is perfect, we all have struggles and inadequacies. This is one way in which God uses us.

What I've always liked about myself is that I never had a problem speaking my mind. I wasn't timid, nor was I afraid; I simply hated being mistreated and didn't have an issue letting it be known. Aside from myself, I also disliked for people around me to be mistreated. I had no problem standing up for others, especially my family. Family meant the world to me. I've always loved hard, and I would go above and beyond for those I cared about. Nothing about me was passive; I was a straightforward, tell it like it is type of girl. I had no choice; it was either keep quiet and be walked over, or be strong and demand respect. I chose the latter. I remember when I was in junior high school, my mother couldn't afford to buy me a popular shoe. Therefore, I had to settle for something more economical. I was okay with this; I was never the type of child to give my mother a hard time. I was always understanding. In fact, I would tell my mother not to worry about me and to make sure my brothers had what they needed. I never put myself first. I was aware that my mother struggled financially, so I made it my business not to add any extra stress. On the first day of school, I remember having on a pair of shoes that wasn't so popular. Even though these shoes weren't in style, they were all my mother could afford, so I wore them. It didn't take long before some of my classmates noticed them and began talking about me. Embarrassed and not wanting to bring any more attention to my shoes, I brushed it off. I didn't want them knowing that it bothered me. In that moment, I was reminded of how ashamed I was. Living off government assistance, Section 8 and food stamps, was embarrassing and it was my goal not to let anyone find out. Back then, all I could think of was how I couldn't wait until I was old enough to get a job, so I could help my mother out. When I turned 15 years old, I got my very first job at McDonald's. I got some of the things I wanted, but more importantly, I was able to help my mother. One of the ways I helped was in taking care of my baby brother. Although I was his big sister, our age gap placed me in the role of being somewhat of a second mother to him. From helping financially, to guiding him educationally, and even disciplining him at times; I was instrumental in his upbringing. Not only did I play a significant role in my baby brother's life, I was also there for the oldest of my brothers as well. In being their older and only sister, the nurturing role came naturally. Although it wasn't always easy being the oldest, I don't regret any of the sacrifices I made for my brothers. Me being there for them didn't take away from my mother being a phenomenal mother. I was aware of the difficult times we faced and even grateful for the sacrifices my mother made, which is why it was important for me to help as much as I could. She did everything in her power to make sure we were well taken care of, even if it meant she had to go without. Although we didn't have everything we wanted, we had everything we needed, and that is what I grew to appreciate.

I've heard the saying "you never know how strong you are until being strong is your only option". Up until this point, I believed I had gone through some stuff, but the magnitude of what I was about to face made my past storms look like a walk in the park. One day while running errands, my mother started having leg pains and shortness of breath. She immediately drove herself to the hospital. After the doctor ordered several tests, they presented her with the results. They told her she had two brain aneurysms. I was devastated and scared out of my mind. I was familiar with aneurysms, because at the age of twelve, a friend of mine passed away from a brain aneurysm. Based off his outcome and stories I had heard, I was terrified of what this meant for my mother. Brain aneurysms are fatal in about 40% percent of cases, and of those who survive, about 66% suffer from permanent neurological deficit. Additionally, 15% of individuals die before even reaching the hospital. All I could think about is that I was going to lose the most important person in my life; my mother. I didn't understand why this was happening. I questioned God and even pleaded with Him; I was a total wreck. As messed up as I was, I didn't let my mother see it. I had to be strong for her.

It was my first year of graduate school, and although I wasn't sure if I would be able to handle everything I was up against, I believed that God wouldn't have put more on me than He was going to give me strength to bear. My mother had to undergo two brain surgeries at two different timeframes. Those processes were emotional, overwhelming, and heartbreaking. Even though she trusted God to work a miracle in her favor, I could tell she was afraid, and it broke my heart into pieces knowing there wasn't anything I could do to help her. I learned in this moment that when there's nothing left to do, all you can do is pray. 1 Thessalonians 5:17 (KJV) tells us to, "pray without ceasing." My mother didn't give up, I didn't give up, family and friends didn't give up, and most importantly, God didn't give up. Prayer truly works, I am a living testament of this. Both aneurysms were repaired, and even though she will have to live with them for the rest of her life, it's forever a reminder of God's greatness and healing power. My faith was put to the test, but I never stopped believing and trusting in the word of God; He will never leave you nor forsake you (see Hebrews 13:5). God never left my side even in times of doubt. He healed my mother and He alone receives the glory.

The road to recovery was challenging. In hindsight, I know it was nothing but God that I made it through that time in my life. I was a full time graduate student, worked part time, had a practicum, and even worked within a graduate assistantship program. My hands were full, and there weren't enough hours in a day for me to commit to what I had going on personally as well as to devote time caring for my mother, but God made a way. He was there with me every step of the way. He never left my side. Every doctor's visit, and everything else my mother needed, He allowed me to be there. Aside from school and work, my life was completely devoted to my mother and making sure she was cared for. 1 Timothy 5:8 says, "But those who won't care for their relatives, especially those in their own household, have denied the true faith. Such people are worse than unbelievers." No matter how tough it got, I didn't leave my mother's side. Family is one of life's greatest blessings and should always be cherished. I couldn't imagine my life without my mother. Because of God strengthening me, I was able to be there for her while also juggling life itself.

So, I'll ask the question again, "What is it that makes a woman strong?" It's never allowing her circumstances to get the best of her. I didn't choose strong, strong chose me. It's who I am and who I'll always be. The Bible tells us where we are weak, God makes us strong. While I was focused on being the strong one in my family, friendships, and relationships, I wasn't acknowledging the true source of my strength: God. Even though I was strong, the strength I possessed had nothing to do with me, but everything to do with God. I hadn't realized it when I was a young girl, but as I got older, I did.

Those who are strong are viewed as never needing help. People don't worry about us; they feel we can handle our own. Even though this is true, it is also true that even the strongest individuals have moments where they need a shoulder to lean on. Nonetheless, no matter how difficult a situation was, I dealt with it. This is the way I was built. I was a fighter, I was tough, I never gave up. Although I would love to take the credit, it wasn't me. It was all God. Psalm 121:1-2 (KJV) says, "I will lift up mine eyes unto the hills, from whence cometh my help. My help cometh from the Lord, which made heaven and earth." I am strong, because of God. He made me this way. It was all a part of His divine purpose for my life. He knew exactly what my story was going to consist of. Therefore, He specifically and strategically designed me this way. In life, we aren't always accepting of the challenges that come our way, but in my spiritual walk, I've learned to trust God through everything. The Bible says in John 15:16, "You didn't choose me. I chose you. I appointed you to go and produce lasting fruit, so that the Father will give you whatever you ask for, using my name." God chose me, just as He chose you. God specifically handpicks us. Our life experiences are not by accident, they are well planned and thought out by God Himself. He had us in mind from the very beginning. Once you truly understand this, it is then when you will be able to see the tough times for what they really are: stepping stones to reaching your destiny. I can truly say, with every trial and with every test, I've become stronger and wiser, and just a little bit closer to reaching my destiny.

CHAPTER FIVE

Painful Goodbyes

God blesses those who mourn, for they will be comforted.

~Matthew 5:4~

There isn't a person who travels through life without at some point, experiencing the loss of a loved one. Grief is one of life's most difficult challenges. Although it's painful, God doesn't leave us to suffer it all alone. His comfort and peace are always there. Loss and grief affects each of us differently. It's a process that varies from individual to individual. Not only did losing people I love impact me emotionally, it also impacted me spiritually. My faith increased, and it helped me to establish more of a closer relationship with God. Through loss is when I truly understood what it meant to live. We often take for granted the gift of life, not realizing it isn't promised to any of us. Therefore, every second, minute, hour and day should be cherished and lived as though it's the last. When I was younger, I lost several loved ones. However, it wasn't until becoming an adult that losing a loved one impacted me differently. I've lost my aunt, my uncle, and a close friend all to cancer. As painful as it was, it was the strength and comfort of God that helped me make it through. Those losses have forever left an imprint on my heart. I've come to realize that you never completely get over a loss, but with time it does get easier.

Aunt Doris

The passing of my Aunt Doris hit like a ton of bricks. It was the first loss that I felt greatly impacted my entire family. Not only was it tough, it changed our family dynamic. Sometimes, the impact of someone's presence isn't recognized until after they're gone. My aunt's absence greatly shifted things within my family; the distance grew tremendously and before we realized it, we weren't spending time together as a family anymore. There was a major void, and the family never truly healed and bounced back from it. Aside from this, one thing that didn't change was my memory of my aunt, a memory I will forever hold on to. Everyone always said how much I resembled her and could've passed for being her daughter. My aunt could sing, so could I. My aunt had a mouth on her and didn't have a problem standing up for herself, and so did I. My aunt was a well put together woman. Although her hair and makeup were always on point, she was beautiful with or without it. Growing up, I always viewed her as being strong. When she received her cancer diagnosis, that strength I had always seen in her magnified. What started as breast cancer, later progressed to lung cancer and eventually spread to her brain. Nevertheless, she hung in there and refused to give up without a fight. I remember a time she had just gotten out of the hospital and she wanted me to show her how to fill in her eyebrows. Even during the roughest moments of her life, she found the strength to keep doing the things she normally would. She didn't allow her circumstances to change who she was. She fought with everything within her to overcome her battle with cancer. In and out of remission and regardless of how tired she grew, she didn't give up. When the cancer resurfaced for the last time, it appeared to be more progressive than it had in the past. Everything seemed to be moving so fast. From her being placed on hospice, to seeing her health deteriorate day by day; it was unbelievable. What seemed like a bad dream turned out to be a reality. I'm not sure which is the most difficult: watching a loved one slowly pass away or an unexpected death. I suppose the blessing in a slow passing is that God gives us time to mentally and emotionally prepare ourselves. Although we can never truly be prepared for the loss of a loved one, the blessing in it is having the opportunity to say goodbye.

On my aunt's sick bed, I talked to her, read scriptures, prayed with her, and played gospel music. One song I recall us listening to over and over was "I Told the Storm." As she laid there, there was a peace that seem to come over her. During this moment is when I gained acceptance of her transition. The day God decided to call her home is forever a vivid memory. She was surrounded by family, and an overflow of love. I had just finished polishing her finger nails, when a change in her breathing began. Each breath became fainter and fainter. As my family and I watched her take her last breath, emotions filled the room. I was overwhelmed, as I had never witnessed anything like this before, especially regarding someone I loved so dearly. I was hurt, but a part of me was also at peace; she would no longer have to suffer. She was free of the hurt and pain this horrendous disease caused. She fought a good fight and she didn't stop until God said otherwise.

I remember being asked to do her makeup for her home going service. I agreed reluctantly, because quite honestly the thought of death had always terrified me. I've always dreaded having to go to funerals. Dreams, constant thoughts, and even images of the body in the casket would consume me. I couldn't fathom the idea of being around a dead body in that capacity. However, this wasn't just a body; this was my aunt and I knew she wouldn't have wanted it any other way. I was scared out of my mind leading up to that very moment, but when I got in the room with her, those feelings subsided. It was such an indescribable peace and calmness that came over me as I touched her face. Her spirit was with me and in that very moment, I received closure. To this day, I sometimes catch myself in deep thought of her. I then turn on her favorite singer, Anita Baker, and my heart begins to smile. Although

I will never get over her no longer being here physically, the memories she left behind will always live in my heart.

Uncle Wayne

What I've always admired about Uncle Wayne was how much he loved his daughters. Born and raised in Memphis, Tennessee, Uncle Wayne embodied a true southern gentleman. It was reflected in the way he talked and in how he carried himself. He contributed so much laughter and positivity to our family that his death produced a huge void. He was the type of person everyone loved to be around. You would hardly ever catch him in a bad mood, he was truly a good person with a heart of gold; this is what I remember most about him. When I learned of him having cancer, I remember saying to myself, "Here we go again." It hadn't been too long since the passing of Aunt Doris and now this. A part of me felt as though my family was being chipped away bit by bit. Witnessing the disease slowly defeat him felt as though I was reliving my aunt's death. Nonetheless, I remained positive and hopeful.

Uncle Wayne and I talked often, whenever he needed me, I was there. As time went by, the cancer progressed. It was heartbreaking seeing the effect it had on him. He was suffering, and there wasn't anything anyone could do to help him. Like always, the only thing I knew to do was to pray. Some people's perception of prayer is that whatever you pray for, God will give you. But what happens in those times when what you pray for, God doesn't give you? I prayed vigorously for God to heal my uncle, but He didn't. Does that mean God doesn't answer prayers or wasn't listening to mine? Not at all, what it means is that it wasn't in God's will. God always knows best. Therefore, He knew what was best for Uncle Wayne. It wasn't my place to question God's decision, it was my place to trust it.

I remember one day he called and said he needed some pajamas. I went to the store and planned to take the pajamas to him the next day. However, I didn't know that would be the last conversation I would have with him. He passed away the very next day while I was at church. I was completely devastated. I didn't get a chance to say goodbye or take him his pajamas as I said I would. I thought I had just a little bit more time, but it was too late; he was gone. As difficult as his passing was, I knew it was for the best; he would no longer have to suffer. Paul says in 2 Corinthians 5:8 (KJV), "We are confident, I say, and willing rather to be absent from the body, and to be present with the Lord." There's a specific type of peace within this scripture, the kind of peace that only God can give. I believe that Uncle Wayne found peace in the presence of the Lord, and because of it, I found peace in knowing he was okay. One thing that's for sure: life is not promised. One minute we are here and then the next we are gone. Understanding this has helped me to appreciate the gift of life and cherish each moment as the blessing it is.

David

David's death hurt me to the core. I was greatly affected by my Aunt Doris and Uncle Wayne's death, but this was different. I think it was because he was so young and hadn't truly lived out his life. David and I had a connection. Although he was my childhood boyfriend, he was more than that. He was my friend. We grew up together, our families were close, and over the years had become like family. His battle with cancer was heartbreaking. Aware that anyone at any age could receive a cancer diagnosis, I just didn't expect it to happen to him. I remember when I first learned the news, I received a call from his mother. Mrs. Farrow and I have always been close since I met David at the age of 13. She would always keep me in the loop regarding how he was doing. Although there were times throughout the span of our friendship that we would talk regularly, there were also times our contact was minimal. But no matter what, we always managed to keep in touch. Our friendship was genuine, and we always remained the same with one another. David was strong and hardly ever revealed a vulnerable side. He wouldn't have dared called to tell me about him being sick. Knowing this about him, I immediately called to check on him. Typical David, he simply said not to worry about him, that he was okay. I followed his advice and didn't worry, instead I prayed. Knowing he needed to take his mind off his circumstance, I didn't bring up the topic of him being sick much. Instead, we reminisced on the good times.

David was a ladies' man back in the day; he was popular, a very good basketball player, a great dresser, and drove a nice car. We had some good laughs recalling our teenage years. Bringing up those memories brought a smile to his face. I could tell it was needed to lighten the mood and take his mind off what he was going through.

Early one Sunday morning, my phone rang. It was David's sister saying he had passed away. I was crushed. Even though it was expected, it was one of the hardest losses I've experienced. I was hurt and devastated, but I eventually realized what I had gained, great memories and an even greater friend. The memories we shared could never be erased or forgotten and I am grateful for the time God allowed me to have with him. Our friendship has left an imprint on my heart and it will forever be cherished.

When someone is older, death may affect them differently than when they're younger. As a child, I really didn't understand death and all it entailed. The emotions that accompany it are sometimes difficult for a child to comprehend. Although I've lost many people throughout my lifetime, it wasn't until becoming an adult that death had a major impact on my life. From losing grandparents, aunts, uncles, cousins, and friends, grief encompasses a wide range of emotions such as sadness, anger, guilt, regret, among many others. The way someone deals with a loss varies and solely depends on certain aspects; for me it was my faith in God that got me through it. Before becoming saved, my view of death and the way I coped with it was different. What I realized is my relationship with God played a huge role in how I responded to the loss. Having a relationship with God has allowed me to understand death more. As sure as we are born, we are sure to die. We can't escape it, we can't ignore it, it's going to happen. There's a saying, "Give your loved ones their flowers while they can still smell them." We'll never know the extent of someone's time here on earth. We can be here today and gone tomorrow. For this reason alone, we should appreciate and enjoy our loved ones while they're still here.

CHAPTER SIX

I Am Who I Am

*For you created my inmost being; you knit me
together in my mother's womb. I praise you because I
am fearfully and wonderfully made; your works are
wonderful; I know that full well.*

~Psalm 139:13-14 (NIV)~

There's a song by LL Cool J called, "Around the Way Girl."
The lyrics of this song describe a girl who lives in a neighborhood, probably urban. Whether it's being in a relationship or just being friends with her, she is the type of girl guys love to be around. She's confident, down to earth, independent, intelligent, and street smart. She is ultimately someone who is strong and stops at nothing to achieve her goals, even in a male dominating world. As far back as I can remember, I related to her; in fact, I was this girl.

I was sometimes referred to as a "pretty girl," by those who didn't truly know me. However, I wasn't the typical pretty girl; I didn't act according to the stereotype of what a pretty girl was.

Quite honestly, I disliked being referred to by this name. I felt it took away from the more meaningful qualities I possessed, there was more to me. I could hang with a group of girls and feel comfortable, and on the other hand, I could hang with a group of guys and feel just as comfortable. I've always been a super cool/goofy girl, who had a lot of friends, mostly male. I was that go-to-friend; my friends talked to me about any and everything. I was popular, and with popularity came drama. I had my share of experiences with girls who disliked me for no reason at all other than jealousy. Because of this, I found myself in situations where I was forced to defend myself.

When I was in middle school, I got into a fight with a classmate. What started off as a one on one fight, ended with me being jumped by four girls. It's not uncommon for the perception of girls who are pretty to be viewed as being weak. I always felt that girls who were easy on the eyes had to fight ten times harder to prove themselves. Because of the way I looked, people automatically assumed I was stuck up. I was judged and categorized before someone even got a chance to know me. Back then, I didn't understand it; I felt I was the coolest girl anyone could know. Unfortunately, we sometimes judge people before even having a conversation with them. We form opinions based off what we've heard and or what we see. For this reason, I was tried by females and it was mainly because of the way I looked. It wasn't my personality, the way I acted, my attitude, or how I treated someone; it was solely because of my looks. One would think this would diminish as the years passed, but this would follow me even throughout my adult life.

While growing up, I didn't participate in many sports, but the one sport I was involved in and absolutely loved, was track. From the age of nine to my sophomore year in high school, I ran track. I stopped when I developed shin splints and tendonitis, but it wasn't too long after that I picked up a new hobby. I have always had an outgoing personality. My mother would tell me as a child that I was going to Hollywood. This would always make me laugh, but I believe she saw something special in me I hadn't initially seen in myself. She was my biggest supporter. Everything I set out to do she was there encouraging and rooting for me. As a child, we attended Murchison Tabernacle C.M.E. Church. What I enjoyed most was singing in the choir. I wasn't a Whitney Houston, but I had a nice tone, at least I thought. I recall the first time I sang for my mother and father. Sitting on their bed, I sang "It's Alright" by Chante Moore. My parents were shocked to learn that their Piggy, a nickname I was given as a child, could sing. They had no idea. From that point on, my mother and the rest of my family had me singing at all the family gatherings, parties and any chance they got. Any excuse there was to celebrate, we did. Where there was family, there was music. Music brought us together, it was a happy place. I grew up listening to just about every rhythm and blues singer you could think of. From Aretha Franklin and Anita Baker to Johnnie Taylor and Bobby Womack; music played a huge role in my upbringing. In hindsight, it helped me to get through a lot of difficult times. It was my place of peace.

It wasn't until I was a junior in high school when I began to take singing seriously. My friend signed us up for our school's first talent show. We would sing together all the time just for fun, so it only made sense for us to perform in the talent show together. We performed Mya and Sisqo's, "It's All About Me." And when I say we performed, we performed! Everyone loved it, so much that we began performing in other talent shows throughout St. Louis. Back then, no one could've convinced me that I wasn't going to become a famous singer. This is how serious and passionate I was about it. Nonetheless, I would eventually realize God's plan for my life was different.

I absolutely enjoyed my high school years. Those years consisted of an array of memories, both good and bad. It was great being young and free without a care in the world. My mother was tough on me regarding academics. Back then I didn't understand it, but eventually I grew to appreciate it. I made pretty good grades. I remember becoming friends with this guy who sold drugs; he would pay me to do his school work. What I later learned is that he had a crush on me. Although he was interested in me, he never crossed any lines. I believe it was because he ultimately respected me. I never had any issues receiving respect from guys, I believe it was because I always carried myself respectfully. I thank my mother for this. She opened the line of communication regarding boys and sex at an early age. There wasn't anything I couldn't talk to her about.

I still remember one of the first things she ever told me about the opposite sex, "Boys only want one thing and when they get it, they'll move on to the next girl, and don't accept anything from a boy because they will expect something in return." I took heed to these words. Growing up, everyone pretty much knew I wasn't sexually active, which is probably the reason most guys chose to become friends with me instead. Most girls my age were either having sex or talking about having sex, but it was the furthest thing from my mind. Because of the values and morals my mother instilled in me, I chose not to go down that path. Seeing friends either become teenage mothers and/or being used and disrespected by guys, it didn't take long for me to learn that sex wasn't for me.

I've always been the type to learn from other people and their experiences. Because of this, I choose not to engage in certain things. I'm a true believer that not only should we learn from our own experiences, but others' as well. I decided early on in life that I would wait until I was older to have sex and I stood by that decision. It wasn't until my junior year in college at the age of 22 when I lost my virginity. A good girl is the reputation I had. However, I would eventually reach a point where I regretted being a "good girl." I felt as though I missed out on living and doing certain things I should have probably done when I was younger. I only had a few serious relationships. Where most people would applaud this, a part of me wished it was different. I didn't have stories like other women had about different guys they had been with. My stories were boring: nothing exciting at all. I didn't date multiple guys at the same time, even with the heartbreak I endured in my past relationships, I remained faithful and honest. This was who I was as a person. Some of my friends didn't understand it, and thought I was crazy for having this outlook. Nevertheless, I remained true to who I was. I eventually felt my faithfulness and honesty was in vain. It didn't matter if you were the most faithful girl in the world, there would still be guys who wouldn't appreciate it. At a certain point, I felt I should have been like the girls who were unfaithful to guys they dated, but for whatever reason, it just wasn't in me.

While I didn't have clarity regarding some areas in my life, other areas were clear. I always had a heart for helping people, I just didn't know it would carry over into the career path I would choose. I've been blessed in having the capability of easily developing rapport with individuals, and it's all because I truly care about people and their wellbeing. For this reason, it was inevitable for me to become a social worker. This was the beginning of me understanding my purpose. A first-generation college student was a huge deal. But to also earn a master's degree was an even greater accomplishment. Mainly because it wasn't my norm or what I grew up around. To be honest, I didn't think much of college when I was younger. If it wasn't for my mother instilling the importance of education and constantly pushing me, I probably wouldn't have gone. She wanted better opportunities for me than she had for herself. I'm forever grateful for her pushing me and not allowing me to settle.

God makes each of us different, and for a specific reason: different paths, upbringings, personalities, choices and experiences. We are different. There's a reason God made me the way I am. Back then I didn't realize it, but as I got older it began to make perfect sense. According to the Bible, David was a man after God's heart. His story included both successes and failures. He wasn't a perfect man, but he had a heart for God. Even with the mistakes he made, he had a deep desire to follow God's will and do everything God wanted him to do (see Acts 13:22). I eventually recognized the heart I had for God. Like David, I wanted to please God, even at young age. I have always had a strong reverence for God. I wanted to do what was right and when I didn't, I immediately felt bad. When I would mess up, fall off, and not live according to His will for my life, I felt horrible. All along I thought it was my guilty conscious, but it was the Holy Spirit convicting me. God has a purpose for each of us, and He specifically develops us into what He desires us to be. At a point in my life, I was trying to be someone God hadn't intended for me to be. Once I accepted God's will for my life, I began to understand myself and God more. Where my focus was once on the wrong things, it shifted; and that's when my relationship with God began to grow.

Believe it or not, no two people are the same. Each of us are uniquely made. From personality traits to physical appearance, we are not the same. What's most important, is that God made us in His own image. This means He loves us so much to allow us to share in His creation. To God we are special, and we were created to fulfill a purpose designed by Him. Who we are has nothing to do with us, but everything to do with God. The moment we begin to get closer to Him, is when we will begin to learn who we really are and what our true purpose in this life is.

CHAPTER SEVEN

The Representative

Whoever walks in integrity walks securely, but he who makes his ways crooked will be found out.
~Proverbs 10:9 (NIV)~

When I first met my husband, the year was ending and a new one was beginning. For many, a new year symbolizes a fresh start. I must say it was just that. The chemistry between us was strong and he gained my interest where other guys hadn't. I've always been selective when involving relationships. I've never been a serial dater or eager to jump in a relationship just for the sake of it. I am very picky, always have been. Even the smallest thing has the capability of turning me off from a person. Surprisingly, I immediately took a liking to him. We hit it off quickly. I've never believed in the whole cliché of love at first sight. However, this is exactly how I would describe the connection we shared. I remember our first date, we talked for hours until the restaurant closed with us being the only two people there. Before I knew it, our first date turned into me inviting him to church the very next day and us spending each day together thereafter.

During this time in my life, I was not looking for a relationship. I was enjoying learning more about myself and focusing on a closer relationship with God. Undeniably, there was something between us. Something rather special that just couldn't be ignored even if I tried to. I had to ask myself if this was love or just a strong liking. Was it possible to fall in love in such a short period of time? Nonetheless, I liked what I was feeling. Excited, I embraced it. I was treated well, I was courted, and chivalry was not dead in our relationship. Car doors were opened and closed, phone calls throughout the day were made just to check on me, "thinking of you" text messages were sent, unexpectant dates, flowers and pretty much all the things that pertained to wooing a woman I had experienced while dating my husband. We were inseparable, and I was without a doubt smitten by him. The attention I received and the effort he put toward the relationship, without me having to do anything, showed his level of interest in me. Was this too good to be true or was this truly a blessing from God? These thoughts raced through my mind. However, I was happy, I mean truly happy. The connection between us wasn't forced, it was natural, and it felt right.

Things moved so fast, before I knew it he was on one knee asking me to be his wife. We had only been dating six months, I couldn't believe we were engaged to be married. All I know is in that moment everything felt right. There was no doubt,

I truly believed everything was happening the way it was supposed to. However, six months after us being engaged I was hit with the unexpected. The last thing a woman wants to discover, especially while planning to get married. He had been sending inappropriate texts to a girl he had a past sexual relationship with. He denied it going any further and being that I didn't have proof of anything physical, I chose to believe him. Even though a part of me felt there was more to the story, I chose to let it go and move forward. We all are familiar with the saying, "When it rains, it pours." Well, I had no idea that a major storm was headed my way. Let's just say, everyone has a representative and sooner or later their true character will eventually surface.

CHAPTER EIGHT

Am I My Sisters Keeper?

> *Be devoted to one another in love. Honor one another above yourselves.*
>
> *~Romans 12:10 (NIV)~*

One day, I received flowers at my job. Not surprised, because it was quite often that my fiancé would send them. As I began to read the card, I realized they were not from him. The card implied that there was another girl he was involved with. Immediately after the flowers, I received a phone call to my job from an anonymous number. While laughing, a female voice asked, "Did you get the flowers?" Before I could respond, she hung up. I immediately called my fiancé, who pretended to be oblivious to what had occurred. Later that evening, I received a call from another stranger, an older woman who I didn't know. This woman stated she was the aunt of the girl who had sent the flowers. Confused as to why she would be calling me and how she even got my number, I simply asked her. She stated my fiancé asked her to call me. Even more confused, she informed me that she had known my fiancé for a long time, because of her being friends with his family. This woman was very nice and respectful, therefore; I decided to listen to what she had to say. The conversation between us was very vague. It was as if she wanted to say something without saying it. She stated she told her niece not to get involved with him. She then apologized for her niece and daughter sending flowers to my job, and the conversation ended.

That same day, I overheard my fiancé's father telling someone that cheating comes along with the territory and that I needed to accept it. I believe his father felt it was a privilege for me to be with his son. I guess it was because of him being a well-known politician. However, I couldn't believe what I was hearing. To my face, he pretended to like me and support my relationship with his son, but behind my back it was the total opposite. What he didn't know about me was that I wasn't weak-minded nor was I fascinated by status and popularity. In hindsight, he should have been happy in knowing his son was blessed to have a woman of great character and value by his side. It's unfortunate that there are people in this world who allow status to define who they are; these people are out of touch with what life is truly about.

The next morning when I arrived at work, I received an email from another female, the girl's cousin. Not only did these three girls go to the extreme of finding out where I worked, they also began sending emails to my job. Was it this serious? Whatever happened to an old-fashioned phone call? The flowers, card, playing on my work phone and emails were a bit much and very immature. For the life of me, I couldn't understand why they chose to go to this extreme to reveal something to me. The situation had nothing to do with anyone but the girl and my fiancé, so why on earth were all these other parties involved? I figured the girl he was involved with was young and immature, so much that she was incapable of handling her own matters and had to solicit the help of her relatives. She simply needed back up. But what these girls didn't know is that they were dealing with a child of God, and God was all the backup I needed. I was determined to allow God to fight this battle. After reading the email from one of the cousins, the pieces started coming together. However, I still needed clarity. I wanted to hear it from my fiancé's mouth that he was involved with this girl. I remember calling and telling him to meet up with me. When he arrived, I had him call the girl's aunt. Since he decided to involve her by having her call me, I felt it was necessary for him to call her. Besides, she seemed like the only person who had some integrity in this whole situation. In that conversation, he was forced to come clean. I say forced, because he didn't willingly offer any sort of a sensible explanation. He was reluctant to tell the whole truth. He told bits and pieces, but the aunt encouraged him to be honest. This lady was fully aware of the situation, yet she wanted him to man up and take responsibility for his actions. As I sat there waiting to hear from him, the words finally came out of his mouth that he had been having sex with this girl. Crushed, I called off the engagement.

Later that day, the aunt called asking if she could pray for me. This one conversation led to various conversations between the two of us. She was honest and open, and even shared some of her life's experiences with me. She encouraged me to seek God before totally walking away. Overwhelmed, I couldn't really process anything. I just listened. Throughout our conversations, she informed me that the relationship my fiancé had with her niece wasn't serious, and her niece was fully aware of us being engaged. She then said my fiancé told her, as well as her niece, that he wanted to be with me and didn't want to continue anything further with her. Because of this, her niece lashed out at me. It's typical of a man that once he gets what he wants, he no longer has any use for a woman. He used this girl. Don't get me wrong, I didn't feel sorry for her, because she consented to be a side chick. However, a part of me was disappointed in the lack of sisterhood; there wasn't a moment where she felt any guilt or remorse for playing a part in the cause of another woman's pain. She was willing to keep it going if he was. It took him ending things between them for her to contact me. Why is it this way? The other woman is content with playing her position if she's getting what she wants, even if it's only a piece of the man. However, as soon as things change, and the relationship ends, it is then that she discovers some integrity and informs the wife, the fiancé, or the girlfriend.

I was devastated. So many emotions had overcame me at once. My issue was not so much with the girl as it was with my fiancé. She didn't owe me anything, her loyalty was not to me. However, a part of me was disappointed, because we as women should support one another, not tear each other down. Men get away with doing these things, because women allow it. They protect men in their wrongdoings. To add more insult to injury, I eventually learned these girls and I were a part of the same sorority. I was disgusted, because this is not the principles our sorority had been built upon. They were not upholding the values of our sisterhood. It was even more disheartening that they would attack an innocent woman over a man, and not just any man, but a man she knew was engaged to be married. I believe this girl thought she was going to be successful in getting him to leave me for her, and even stood by in hopes that this would transpire. Realistically, men will tell a woman anything to get what they want, even if it means lying and having her believe he's going to leave his woman. It's not about what they tell you more so than you allowing this to be an option to begin with.

The Bible speaks against fornication and there's a vital reason behind it. During sex, a transfer of spirits take place. This is why God only intended for sex to be between husband and wife (see 1 Corinthians 7:2). When you have sex with someone God has not connected you to, it can become a recipe for disaster. Misguided emotions, hurt, guilt, anger, and resentment are some of the factors that may be the result of fornication. When we make choices out of the will of God, we expose ourselves to unnecessary drama and pain. This is exactly what took place. This girl grew attached to a man who God intended for someone else. It wasn't because of the nonexistent dates he took her on, the nonexistent quality time they spent together, or the nonexistent thoughtful things he did for her. It was simply because of sex. A three-letter word that has the power of destroying relationships, causes men to be tempted, and allows women to believe it's acceptable to be a side chick. The moment he ended things is when she realized their sexual relationship wasn't enough to make him commit to her. Women so often think that sex is enough to keep a man. It's true that it will get you a man, but the furthest thing from the truth is that it will keep that man. Her anger was directed toward the wrong person; her issue was not with me, it wasn't even with him: it was with herself. She made the decision to accept being the other woman. She knew what her role was from the very beginning and therefore she had no one to blame but herself. Unfortunately, some people aren't mature enough to hold themselves accountable for their actions. So, they blame others. Although I held my fiancé totally accountable for what he had done, part of me was saddened by the reality that women upholding one another hardly exists. Even though she and I didn't know one another, and she didn't owe me anything, we are women and that alone is enough to support, respect, and honor one another.

CHAPTER NINE

The Decision

Trust in the Lord with all your heart, and lean not on your own understanding. In all your ways acknowledge Him, and He will make straight your paths.
~Proverbs 3:5-6 (ESV)~

Imagine going through a tough situation and those closest to you have no idea about it. I was ashamed, and that shame caused me to keep it to myself. I was silently suffering. The few people who were aware of my situation were very supportive. My mother of course, was one of those people. Although she was upset about what occurred, mainly because of the pain it caused me, she offered wise and sound advice. She assured me that whatever decision I were to make, she had my back. Even though it was up to me how I would proceed, I just didn't have a clue of what that consisted of. But I eventually had to figure it out.

Even with the support I had, I still felt alone. Maybe this was all a part of God's plan. Ultimately, all I needed was God anyway.

God will sometimes get us by ourselves, where we are focused only on Him and where it's easier for us to hear from Him without any outside distractions. I wanted to hear from God regarding what to do, so I prayed and consulted with my pastor. With time moving fast and our wedding date approaching, I still hadn't received clarity on how to move forward. Maybe it was because I was focused on the wrong things. Truthfully, I was more concerned with the embarrassment than the lifetime commitment and didn't want to deal with everything that came along with calling off a wedding. In life, we are likely to experience some level of embarrassment. Some embarrassment we may cause, while others, we may not. What I've come to learn is that it's not about what people say and think about your situation that matters, it's what you think. It's how you use the situation to become better, stronger, and allow yourself to grow from it. Although I was praying over my situation, I can truly admit my focus wasn't completely on God and what He wanted for me. I was entirely consumed by the situation and I eventually realized that it was because I was trying to control my circumstances instead of allowing God to. When we encounter tough times and we decide to take it to God, we are saying to God that it's too much for us to handle and we are asking for Him to take control. In making this request, we must totally let go. So often we find ourselves holding on and still trying to have some sort of control. Giving it to God simply means just that. I hadn't done this and therefore, I found myself eventually having to deal with the result of not truly seeking God.

My decision to either move on with my life or give my fiancé another chance wasn't easy. Even though I said to him many times that the relationship was over, he was adamant and persistent in not giving up. My decision was overshadowed by my emotions as well as the lack of space I received from him. I can honestly say, had he gone on about his business and did as I asked, it would have made my decision to let go of the relationship easier. However, it didn't happen this way. The ultimate factor in deciding to give the relationship a chance was solely based upon one aspect; our relationship didn't consist of sex. Before meeting my fiancé, I was celibate. I made a commitment to God that I would do things the right way, His way. Since I had waited to adulthood to become sexually active, I felt waiting to marriage is what I initially should have done. Because I was maturing spiritually, it was important for me to recommit myself to God. I no longer wanted to give myself to a boyfriend, so I decided the next person I would become intimate with would be my husband. I truly believed in doing this, God was going to bless and have favor over our union. When I initially discussed my standards and expecta-tions with my fiancé, he respected it. Aware that sex was not an option until after marriage, he made it clear that moving forward in pursuing a relationship with me is what he wanted. Because he and I hadn't been intimate with one another, it caused me to be more accepting in the possibility of giving the relationship a chance. Ultimately, I considered where he was spiritually. He wasn't saved and prior to knowing me he hadn't had the desire to be. Although I had been celibate for quite some time now, I couldn't expect the same of him. Truth is, I was further along spiritually than he was, and therefore I chose to be more realistic in my view. In addition to loving him and him proving how sincere he was about the mistakes he made, I decided to proceed with marriage. Was this the right decision? This very question would someday resurface.

CHAPTER TEN

The Wilderness

Behold I am doing a new thing; now it springs forth,
do you not perceive it? I will make a way in the
wilderness and rivers in the desert.
~Isaiah 43:19 (ESV)~

The "wilderness experience" is often viewed as a period in a believer's life where they experience tough times and trials. The purpose behind this experience is to be developed. Although distress, doubt, and alienation from God possibly occur here, this is where God specifically places us, so we can be transformed. For me, it was one of the worst times of my life. In addition to the common stresses that life brings, I was in the beginning stages of regretting being married. My idea of marriage was totally different than what I was experiencing. My husband did not have my back and wasn't being the protector as I expected him to be. I was disappointed, because here I am, a married woman having to defend and protect myself. Shockingly, never did I imagine needing defending and protecting from my husband's own father. The level of disrespect and mistreatment I received from this man was something I had never experienced in my entire life. Not only was the disrespect directed toward me, it was also toward my husband. It was reflected in the way he spoke to him, his behavior toward him, and even how he treated me. Although his father's true character began to surface early on, nothing could have prepared me for what was to come.

During this period in my life, I felt alone with no way out. I couldn't talk to my husband; he was biased and didn't understand. I couldn't talk to my family, because I didn't want them to dislike my husband for not standing up for me. The few friends I did share my situation with were very supportive, however it still didn't change anything. I was lost and didn't know in what direction I was headed. I was in a spiritual desert. I felt as though God had forgotten all about me. No matter how hard I prayed and how many spiritual leaders I reached out to for advice and guidance, nothing changed. My faith was unstable; I was vulnerable, angry, and hopeless. Although some storms we encounter in life last longer than others. At certain times, we can see a glimpse of the sun peeking through, giving us an inkling of hope. However, this was no ordinary storm. It lasted for several years getting worse and worse, not seeming as if it was ever going to end. My days were as dark as my nights and the possibility of sunshine seemed impossible. What I eventually decided to do was shift my focus from *what* was happening to me, to *why* it was happening. As much as everything around me was in shambles, I had to realize I was right where God wanted me. There was a message within the mess I was going through, and although I felt it was grand, it was not the bigger picture. It was just a tiny intricate piece of the puzzle and in due season, its purpose would be manifested.

In the wilderness, we should be encouraged and reminded that God can do all things but fail. For example, Jesus was in the wilderness for forty days. He fasted and was tempted by the devil three times, but remained faithful to God's will for His life (see Matthew 4:1-11). God could have left Jesus there all alone to be consumed by the enemy, but He didn't. He equipped Jesus with what He needed to make it out. Another example is the children of Israel, because of their disobedience and lack of belief in God's word and promises, He allowed them to wander in the wilderness for forty years (see Numbers 32). God will keep us in the wilderness however long it takes for Him to achieve His purpose in us. In my case, God was changing certain things within me, and even though I complained about how long I had been suffering and all that I had been going through, it was all a part of my process. I was being renewed, reformed, and transformed. My faith was being tested, and even though I said I trusted God and even believed I did; the truth is that I wasn't completely trusting in Him. I was trusting Him for some things; but this process was teaching me to trust in Him for all things. In addition to learning to wholeheartedly trust God, I was also learning patience and being in control: an area in which I've always struggled in. Things don't always go according to our plan and on our schedule, and even in the most distressed time of my life, I had to learn to wait on God and do things His way. Isaiah 40:31 (KJV) says, "But they that wait upon the LORD shall renew their strength; they shall mount up with wings as eagles; they shall run, and not be weary; and they shall walk, and not faint." Patience was a struggle for me, and because of this, God was teaching me what it means to wait on Him. In addition to this, He also placed me in a position to understand that it isn't me who has control over my life, but that He's in total control. As Christians we must understand that our lives are not our own, they belong to God, and therefore what we do is not for our own benefit, but for God to receive the glory. The prophet Jeremiah understood this clearly when he prayed, "I know, LORD, that our lives are not our own. We are not able to plan our own course," (Jeremiah 10:23). In understanding this, we can begin to look at the stuff we go through differently and with unwavering confidence in God.

Early on in my story, I mentioned that I never had any problems speaking my mind. Well this was one of the areas God wanted to change in my life. I realized that although having the boldness to stand up for myself and speak my mind may be a good quality; there's always a time and place for it. Where I should have been using wisdom, I wasn't. Every battle wasn't designed for me to fight, sometimes I simply needed to give it to God. Even when my husband wasn't standing up for me and even when I was being disrespected and mistreated by his father, I only needed to allow God to fight for me. It wasn't my place to correct my husband for what he was or wasn't doing, this was God's place. As women, the Bible tells us to have a gentle and quiet spirit (see 1 Peter 3:4). Because this was an area I needed some major work in, God began to deal with me. In addition to the many lessons God placed before me throughout my wilderness experience, His sovereign power was the most vital. There's absolutely nothing impossible with God, and although I had been told this and even believed it, I was in the process of living it and experiencing it for myself.

While God was rearranging several areas within my life, my place of worship began to shift. My former pastor is without a doubt a great man of God, and has always been very supportive. I also enjoyed worshipping and fellowshipping at my former church home. No one could have ever told me I wouldn't be a lifetime member. I was active and had developed some great friendships, but I was complacent. Sometimes God takes us out of our comfort zone to develop us. This is exactly what was happening in my life. God had been dealing with me for over a year, and although I ignored it, deep down I knew I wasn't progressing spiritually. God was simply saying it was time to move. I'd like to compare spiritual elevation to levels of education. First, you attend preschool and then elementary school. Once completing elementary school, you advance on to junior high school and then high school. After passing the high school level, you graduate and go off to college or the next level of your education. The same thing happens during our spiritual walk. There are different levels and within each level, we walk away with more knowledge than we did the previous one. It's all a part of the growth process. Although I didn't know where I was going to end up, I trusted God. I left my church and began visiting other churches and learned some vital lessons along the way.

Although I had visited a few churches, I had yet to encounter a church in which I felt I was led by God. The feeling of not belonging to a church home weighed heavy on me. In addition to feeling lost regarding other areas of my life, not having a church home brought on a feeling of incompleteness. Some people believe that if you believe in God, read the Bible, are charitable, watch religious television programs on Sunday and you are a good person, that you don't need to attend church. This is a huge misconception. Being Christ-like is doing the same things Christ did. Jesus attended church and fellowshipped with other believers. Therefore, there's no way we can be Christ-like and not do the same things Christ did. About a year had passed and I still hadn't found a church home. I started to feel as though my walk with God was in limbo. I was discouraged and frustrated. As frustrated as I was, it was important for me to be where God wanted me. Therefore, I remained patient.

In my patience, God lead me to Open Door Christian Center. I recall the very first time I visited, I instantly judged it. I was there for a women's revival and although the revival was good, I couldn't get past what the building used to be. It wasn't the typical traditional church I had experienced. Therefore, I wasn't open to the possibility of this being the place God intended for me to be. After coming up with every reason in my mind why this church wasn't for me, the Holy Spirit led me right back there. What started off as me judging the outside before actually experiencing what was on the inside, turned out to be a great blessing. For a year, I was in search of being a part of a ministry that consisted of an intimate setting, a place I could grow spiritually, where I would feel free in my worship, where my gifts would be utilized, and ultimately a place where the spirit of God dwells. God answered my prayers and from this point on, my walk with God progressed. I was on a new journey and allowing God to use me in ways I never imagined. Right before my eyes, I was becoming a different person.

Satan's overall goal is to kill, steal, and destroy; what better time to manipulate someone than when they're weak, vulnerable and weary? The wilderness is Satan's perfect opportunity for this to take place. His primary purpose is to get us to doubt God and to serve him instead. Like he did when Jesus was in the wilderness, Satan will tempt us with things that appear to be good for us as a way of getting us to turn our backs to God. In hindsight, we wouldn't experience the wilderness if God doesn't allow it. God will never lead us where His grace cannot provide for us or His power cannot protect us. There's a purpose for everything we go through. God knows the purpose and so does Satan. Ever wondered why when people give their lives to God and start living right that the enemy begins to attack? This is because Satan is threatened by spiritual progress. Many people think that the moment a person becomes saved, that it's smooth sailing. This is untrue. Satan will try to do everything he can to get you off track with God. His intent is to destroy us in the wilderness, where God's intent is to develop us through it.

There is absolutely no way you can avoid the wilderness. It's a road we all must travel. It may take place in the form of depression, a crisis, or a span of traumatic life events. Although it's not a joyful time, the wilderness is not a time where we are being punished, it's a time where we are being positioned. Even though I felt all alone and that know one really understood what I was dealing with, I learned that I experienced this place of isolation because God was preparing me for something only He and I would understand. This experience wasn't about anyone but me and God. In my most desolate moment, God was right there by my side. Even in the wilderness, He was there.

CHAPTER ELEVEN

Sleeping With The Enemy

For husbands, this means love your wives, just as
Christ loved the church. He gave up his life for her.
~Ephesians 5:25~

Marriage is more than a man and woman becoming one flesh, it's a representation of the relationship between Christ and the Church. In marriage, husbands are to love their wives as they love themselves. The word of God states in Ephesians 5:29 (ESV), "For no one ever hated his own flesh, but nourishes and cherishes it." It's vital for husbands to truly understand what it means to love their wives as themselves so that the marital standards set by God are fulfilled. Additionally, Ephesians 5:22-23 says, "For wives, this means submit to your husbands as to the Lord. For a husband is the head of his wife as Christ is the head of the church. He is the Savior of his body, the church." What happens when a husband doesn't honor his marriage, doesn't love his wife as he loves himself, and isn't leading the marriage in the right direction? The submissiveness and respect a wife should have for her husband may be affected. Undeniably, we all are held accountable for the things we do. Regardless of what your spouse does or does not do, God's expectation of someone upholding their role as husband or wife isn't contingent upon if the other is fulfilling their commitment or not. This was an area in which I greatly struggled in.

I've always taken marriage seriously, and therefore it was important for me to uphold my role as a wife. However, I was reluctant to because my husband wasn't doing the same. Was I biblically justified? No. Nonetheless, this was my truth and I could no longer give my all to a marriage when it wasn't being reciprocated. I refused to be led by my husband when I felt he was leading our marriage straight to hell. I had reached my breaking point and I never imagined being in a place where I felt my husband was my enemy. However, this was my reality. I was emotionally and mentally drained. The respect was gone, the trust was gone, being in love was nonexistent, and the loyalty was nowhere to be found. It was bad, I mean really bad. How did we get here? This was the question that constantly ran through my mind; but more importantly, how long would we be here? Would things get better or would we eventually divorce and go our separate ways? As much as I wasn't fond of divorce, I wasn't fond of staying in an unhealthy marriage either. Through several counseling attempts and even separating at a point, nothing changed. Things only worsened.

I knew I deserved better, more than what he was giving me and later realizing, more than he was even capable of giving.

For the longest time, I was under the impression our marriage was private and we kept others out of our business. I eventually learned I was the only one honoring this agreement. My husband had absolutely no regard for our marriage. He talked about me to others and even allowed them to do the same. He communicated to others his feelings toward me and our marriage, yet refused to inform me. He treated me like I was an enemy, as if I wasn't his partner. He opened the door for others, primarily his family, to have an input on our marriage. Here I am, a wife protecting and respecting her marriage while all along my husband had been telling people just about everything we were going through. He gave people an open invitation, a front row seat into our lives. They commented on it, had an opinion on it, influenced him negatively, and even planted bad seeds. They had the upper hand. As a wife, this was the most horrible feeling. Considering how much of a private person I've always been, it angered me. I hated the fact people knew of the issues my husband and I were experiencing, especially those who were against it and wasn't offering spiritual guidance. I had pretty much given up hope.

As I shared before, I asked myself, "How did we get here?" I can honestly say, we were unequally yoked. We were not on the same page nor level spiritually and mentally. When I first met my husband, he wasn't saved. However, him not having a relationship with God initially wasn't an issue for me, we all have things we need to work on. What mattered is that he believed in God, eventually became saved, and worked toward establishing a close relationship with Him. Ever since our first date, he had been attending church consistently. As time went on, I began feeling that the only reason he was going to church was because he knew that's what I wanted. I later learned he was a different person when he wasn't around me. The way he talked and the things he did were different. At this point, I didn't know who I was married to. I felt lost and misled. Our definition and expectation of marriage differed in so many ways. Bluntly put, my husband had some maturing to do, and because of this, our marriage suffered. There's a saying, "When you know better, you do better." My husband didn't know what being a husband consisted of.

As I began to reflect, I wondered why I failed to see the bigger picture. Truthfully speaking, I've never been the type who jumped at the first opportunity I got to get married. It wasn't a situation where I looked past all the mess just because I wanted badly to be married. I've never been desperate, never been insecure, and never had problems in the dating department. I've always had standards and made them very clear from the very beginning. Therefore, it was mind boggling that I ended up here. Marriage wasn't initially on my agenda while my husband and I was dating. It was something he brought up. He pursued it and because I loved him and felt he was the one, I accepted. Scripture tells us: he who finds a wife, finds a good thing. My husband found me, not the other way around.

But I couldn't understand why he wanted to get married if he wasn't ready. In hindsight, I believe he truly thought he was prepared for marriage based off what he felt it consisted of, but later realized he bit off more than he could chew. I admit, I am a tough cookie. I know what I want, what I deserve, and I don't stand for just anything. I could have overlooked a lot of things my husband was doing; however, I knew better, and I ultimately wanted better from him.

Aside from how I was being treated, I was good to my husband, even when I felt he didn't deserve it. But this approach began to run thin, I was tired of being good to him when he wasn't being good to me. I began to resent him based upon how he was treating me. Intimacy hardly existed, and when it did there wasn't a connection. As bad as it may sound, the reality was that I dreaded being intimate with my husband. I'm not just referring to sex, any type of affection was a struggle for me. All I could think of was how he treated me, lied to me, and failed to protect and defend me. There was a strong disconnect, and my feelings were no longer in it. I had emotionally checked out. Reaching a point of great unhappiness and bitterness, I stopped putting forth any effort. I was done. At one point, I remember wishing he would cheat so I could have biblical grounds for a divorce. It was this bad, I pretty much wanted out. However, it's important to be careful what you wish for, you just may get it. Aside from this, I also wanted to be in the will of God. Quite frankly, I wavered between pleasing my flesh and pleasing the spirit. The spiritual aspect was more important, it's what allowed me to hang in there the length of time I did.

Despite everything that was going on in my marriage, I wanted to please God. Although I didn't succeed in every area, I put forth effort. Deep inside I truly wanted and hoped things would get better, but I didn't think it was possible. So much had occurred and honestly, I didn't think we could make it through. Don't get me wrong, I trusted God and I believed there's nothing impossible for Him; but I thought God didn't want us together to begin with. I felt that because I married him too quickly and ignored the warning signs, that God was punishing me. I prayed and prayed, sought spiritual advice and did everything I knew to do; yet nothing changed.

At the beginning of our marriage, my husband was the sweetest person. He was thoughtful, caring, and fun to be around. We had a good time together, but eventually it all changed. His true colors began to surface. The things he had been used to doing and getting away with in the past, he wasn't able to do with me. My husband couldn't just walk all over me. And because of this, we bumped heads. Prior to him meeting me, he never really experienced someone telling him when he was wrong. He had never been held accountable for his actions, and therefore he resisted constructive criticism. When addressing issues or concerns I had within our marriage, he would instantly shut down and become defensive. His unwillingness to effectively communicate greatly contributed to our marriage reaching its downfall.

The friction between us was so strong, almost unbearable. He hardly ever saw a problem with anything he would do; and if he did, he would make promises that things would get better only for it to continue happening. One of our main issues was the lying. My husband struggled with being honest. He would lie over the smallest things. I have always despised lying. In fact, one of the qualities I love about myself is my honesty. Of all the flaws or shortcomings my husband could have possessed, it happened to be the one I hated most. I even thought to myself that maybe God was teaching me something. Maybe He was teaching me patience. It also didn't help that my husband worked within a career that was sometimes known to involve dishonesty. I witnessed the negativity that came with politics, how it presented opportunities for my husband to conflict with other people. There was always a battle. I viewed politics as not being spiritually good for my husband, I felt it was hindering his walk with Christ. In no way am I saying it's impossible to be a Christian and politician, but I do feel that politics wasn't helping him attain a closer relationship with the Lord. Scripture says, "For what is a man profited, if he shall gain the whole world, and lose his own soul?" (Matthew 16:26, KJV). Politics was everything to him; he ate, slept, and breathed it. He genuinely cared about the wellbeing of his constituents and people in general. He was passionate and focused on positively impacting his community. He absolutely loved politics and was great at it, but he placed it above everything. Although I complained about him putting his career first and the strain it had on our marriage, I never expressed to my husband how I felt his career was hindering him spiritually. It was important for me to support him regardless of what my personal feelings consisted of. I understood that it wasn't about me and my will, it was all about God's will being fulfilled in his life.

No matter how tough a situation may become, sometimes it's best to take your hands off it and give it to God. Even though I was in an unhappy and unhealthy marriage, I realized the only one who could fix it was God. Not me, not my husband, and not those who we sought spiritual advice from, but God Himself. Even though I was still in my storm, I had faith it wasn't going to last forever. Therefore, I chose to embrace my circumstances and stand with great expectancy. God was up to something and whatever it was, I was going to be ready.

CHAPTER TWELVE

Enough is Enough

> Behold, I have given you authority to tread on
> serpents and scorpions, and over all the power of the
> enemy, and nothing shall hurt you.
> *~Luke 10:19 (ESV)~*

Have you ever been fed up, can't take anymore, and if one more thing happens you are going to explode? In life, we are sure to encounter situations that will push us to our limit. Although some people are more capable of enduring certain things for longer periods of time, if pushed, we all will eventually get to a point where enough is enough.

I recall the very first time meeting my husband's father. He asked me my credit score. I didn't receive a, "It's nice to meet you...tell me a little about yourself...how did you and my son meet?" etc. I received a, "What's your credit score?" Caught off guard, and not knowing exactly how to react, I brushed it off. Initially, I figured he just didn't have a filter and didn't mean any harm. Therefore, I chose to overlook it. Soon after, he began to take an interest in the amount of money I earned. Everything was about money and status with him. It wasn't about morals and values, which are the more common and important aspects most parents focus on regarding individuals their children date and marry. It was all about money. At one point he even tried to talk me into signing documents that would prevent me from receiving money from his family's business if my husband and I were to ever divorce. The topic of money was brought up just about every opportunity he got, and I was made to feel as though I wasn't good enough. He displayed a disposition of superiority and looked down on others who didn't have the "things" he and his family had. As much as this bothered me, I ignored it. Eventually, he began planting seeds of doubt by telling me my husband made more money than what he led me to believe. Again, money was the underlying motivator. Although I believe finances are very important, I don't feel it's the most important aspect of life. Regardless if what he was saying was true or untrue, I found it strange for him to communicate this sort of information to me. What I soon learned is he had an agenda to destroy our relationship and would stop at nothing to accomplish this.

After we married, the behavior of my husband's father worsened. In instances where I would normally keep quiet regarding the offensive things he would say and do, I finally decided to discuss it with my husband. My husband's response always resulted in him saying he would address the matter with his father. However, nothing changed. As time went by, the treatment I received became almost unbearable, and instead of standing up and defending myself as I normally would, I chose to keep the peace and tolerate it out of love for my husband. Like me, my husband is very family oriented. Family is everything to him. Most times when he would visit his family I would go with him. Although I was aware there would be a great possibility I would be mistreated by his father, I set my feelings aside to make my husband happy. Because marriage is about sacrifice and compromise, I made the choice to place my peace and happiness on the back burner for my husband's, in hopes that in time things would get better.

As the tension worsened between his father and I, so did the tension between my husband and me. In hindsight, I believe this is exactly what his father wanted. As Christians, we are commanded to honor our mother and father (see Deuteronomy 5:16). Just as we are to uphold this commandment, fathers also have a responsibility not to provoke their children (see Ephesians 6:4). I believe some people feel that just because they are responsible for bringing a person into the world, they are entitled to control their lives. Based upon what I witnessed, my husband's father's controlling ways made it difficult for him to accept the reality: his son was an adult who had started his own family. In him attempting to control our marriage, the conflict between us grew. One way I noticed him controlling people was with money and intimidation. He seemed to always have some sort of conflict and or disrespectful tone toward women. The Bible says,

"Fearing people is a dangerous trap, but trusting the LORD means safety," (Proverbs 29:25). My husband's father was big in size, which can be very intimidating. However, I do not fear man. My confidence resided in knowing God would always protect me. Things eventually got to the point of me having to speak up for myself. From as far as I knew, my husband's approach hadn't changed the situation, and therefore I felt I needed to say something. Once the issue was addressed, I noticed his dislike toward me intensified. I felt that deep down he had an issue with the level of strength I possessed. There are men who simply dislike strong women because of their own weakness and insecurities. In the beginning, when I was ignoring the disrespect I received from him, everything was fine; but the moment I began standing up for myself, it became a problem. People will walk all over you if you allow them to, it's simply your choice as to what you allow in your life and how you allow people to treat you. As for me, I'd much rather have a million-people disliking me for standing up for myself, than being liked for not.

In marriage, God should always be first, your spouse, and then your children. The Bible tells us that when a man marries, he is to leave his mother and father and cleave to his wife and they will become one flesh (see Genesis 2:24, KJV). At this point, all other relationships that were once primary should now become secondary. The meaning behind this scripture is not that a man should disregard his affections to his parents or be in remiss in his honor and respect for them, or even neglect caring for them if they stand in need. But by the order set by God, there is to be more of an intimate connection between husband and wife that it succeeds even between parents and children. Everyone has a position. For instance, a wife can't be a mother to her husband, and a mother can't fulfill the role of a wife to her son. Each person, whether it's husband, wife, mother, father, sister, brother etc., has their own respective role; and until everyone can understand and respect their position, there will always be some level of friction. I've never dated anyone whose family didn't like me, let alone love me, which is why it was so difficult for me to understand why I was having issues with my husband's family. I eventually began to understand that the issue wasn't with me, it was them and their inability of letting go of their son. I say "them" because, even though I considered myself to be close with my husband's mother, it didn't take long for me to discover the relationship wasn't genuine as I believed it to be. Nothing his father had done surprised me, but she appeared to be much different. Although her ways weren't comparable to his, she still wasn't the woman I thought I knew and the woman I had grown to care for. My husband's father made it clear how much he disliked me and didn't want me with his son, while I believed the love she had for me was sincere. Sometimes when you walk into relationships with an open heart, people tend to take advantage of it. I've learned that everyone doesn't value and appreciate genuine people. Although the lesson was hurtful, I am grateful to God for revealing the true substance of that relationship.

As time progressed, I learned my husband's father was overly interested in the relationship between his son and me, and as strange as it may sound; so was he with me. Later down the line, I learned he ran a background check on me. For whatever reason, this man wanted to know more about me than what had already been shared. The moment I realized things were much deeper than what I thought, is when I learned of him reaching out to one of my friends inquiring about my sexual past. The disrespectful and rude comments made toward me, the mistreatment, the lies, and even the background check I was able to look past; but this incident took things to a greater level. When asked about it, his reasoning was since my husband and I made the decision to wait until after marriage to have sex, he suspected I was having sex with someone else. Usually the person who is dating or interested in dating someone would inquire about their sexual past, therefore I found it completely odd and out of order for this man to have an interest in my personal life. I was furious and had never felt so violated.

Of all the things he had done to me, this was the most vile and repulsive. I was greatly offended and couldn't stand the thought of being in his presence. I had never met a person like this in all my life. I was convinced now more than ever, that there had to be some other explanation for his behavior. I asked myself time and time again, "What have I gotten myself into?" A part of me blamed myself, because I should've taken my time before jumping into marriage. I should've truly learned who I was marrying as well as the family I was mar-rying into. However, no matter how much I regretted it and blamed myself, deep down I knew my husband was ultimately responsible for allowing things to get to this point. Although his father was responsible for his behavior, it wouldn't have had the capability of affecting me or our marriage had my husband taken a stand from the very beginning. Because he failed at creating necessary boundaries, our marriage was affected. His family said whatever and did whatever they wanted, and for the life of me I couldn't understand why my husband reacted so nonchalantly. But I learned that just because something seems to be simplistic doesn't mean it really is. My husband was accustomed to his father's behavior. Things had been this way his entire life and therefore, he had grown immune to it. I understand how certain behaviors or environments can become normalized. However, there's a point when adults must make a choice to break away from those dysfunctional behaviors for change to take place.

I've heard the saying that, "When you marry a person, you marry their family too." I think there's a possibility of this saying possessing some truth, but only if there aren't limitations involved. Marriage is a sacred union only between husband and wife. However, when outside influences are allowed inside the marriage, it can result in a husband and or wife feeling as if they are also married to their spouse's family. For this reason, it is important for boundaries to be set, especially when the intent of others may be to destroy the marriage. Although I didn't have the best relationship with my husband's family, I decided to no longer concern myself with it. I understood I didn't marry them, and therefore I could only focus on my marriage. Unfortunately, our marriage wasn't a priority for my husband. As important as it was for us to keep people out of our marriage, my husband had been doing the total opposite. He allowed his parents in our marriage by sharing with them certain things he shouldn't have. In doing this, he did exactly what his father wanted: control. Unsurprisingly, the information my husband shared, his father gossiped to family members, friends, church members, and just about anyone willing to listen. Any opportunity his father got to discredit my character and our marriage, he did. Because of his dislike for me, I believe he wanted others to feel the same way. I understand we live in a time where people are quick to believe a lie over the truth and negative over the positive. However, I had been through enough and the last thing I was going to do was allow what people thought of me to steal my joy. Although some people believed his lies, there were those who knew my character wasn't reflective of the things he had said. Some of my husband's relatives took the time to get to know me for themselves and treated me with respect and kindness despite what they were led to believe. This displayed good character, and I will always appreciate them for it.

Even though I've experienced my share of dysfunction throughout my childhood, nothing compared to what I was currently experiencing. I must admit, I was ashamed. For about the first year of marriage, I hardly mumbled a word about what I was going through. I was so embarrassed, because what I initially thought was going to be a happy uniting of families turned out to be the total opposite. Because of us marrying quickly, I felt people was expecting for the marriage to fail. The embarrassment caused me to hold everything inside and pretend as if I was fine. Initially, I didn't even tell the people closest to me: my family. Although my husband wasn't standing up being what I needed him to be, I didn't want my family's view of him to change. Therefore, I chose to keep it from them for as long as I could. Eventually, things became too much for me to handle and I decided I needed my family's support. Although they were not happy to hear what had transpired, they respected my marriage and continued to show kindness toward my husband. Those close to me wanted to get involved regarding how his father treated me, however, the God in me as well as me wanting to keep the peace, asked them not to. Truthfully, I didn't want to make matters worse. Ephesians 6:12 (KJV) says, "For we wrestle not against flesh and blood, but against principalities, against powers, against the rulers of the darkness of this world, against spiritual wickedness in high places." The battle I was fighting was not natural, but spiritual; therefore, it had to be fought in the spirit.

No matter how tough things got, no matter how people came up against me, no matter how his father continuously slandered my name, told lies about me, disrespected me, threatened me, harassed me, called my job attempting to get me fired, made a flirtatious gesture toward me, and even inquired about my sexual past; I never sought revenge. Although the fighter in me wanted to retaliate, God expected different. The Bible says, "God blesses you when people mock you and persecute you and lie about you and say all sorts of evil things against you because you are my followers. Be happy about it! Be very glad! For a great reward awaits you in heaven. And remember, the ancient prophets were persecuted in the same way," (Matthew 5:11-12). No matter how many lies were told about me or even the many attempts at tarnishing my character, it didn't work. I hadn't understood it at first, but eventually I realized the attacks had nothing to do with me, but everything to do with the God in me.

CHAPTER THIRTEEN

The Ultimate Betrayal

*Give honor to marriage, and remain faithful to one
another in marriage. God will surely judge people
who are immoral and those who commit adultery.*

~Hebrews 13:4~

The last thing a wife wants to discover is that her husband
has been unfaithful. The next to last thing is receiving this
information from someone other than her husband. Well,
this is how I learned of my husband's infidelity. I recall one
morning receiving a text. A guy reached out to a relative of
mine and left his number requesting for me to contact him.
When I saw the message, I instantly knew what it was pertaining to. This was the same guy who reached out to me prior to
my husband and I getting married and who had informed me
of the exchange of text messages he had with a female. I knew
there could only be one reason this guy could be contacting
me, but I only hoped it wasn't true. There's really no way to
prepare yourself for this type of news. Before calling the guy,

I first spoke with my husband. My intent was to allow him the opportunity to shed light on what was going on. I dreaded having to hear anything pertaining to my marriage from someone other than my husband. When asked, my husband denied knowing what the guy wanted, but I knew he wasn't being honest. Therefore, I called the guy.

In our conversation, he informed me that he believed my husband and the mother of his child were sleeping together. He stated he discovered some emails exchanged between them. He also stated that the emails didn't confirm anything sexual, but based off their history, he believed their contact was sexual. To me, it didn't matter if it was sexual or not, it was inappropriate for him to be in contact with someone he had sexual history with. I didn't know if I should believe this guy, but because of my husband's past, I wasn't necessarily doubting this information either. At this point, I had not received anything proving this information to be true. Yes, I could've taken this guys word for it, I could've even taken my husband's word. However, there's this thing called a woman's intuition and I knew there was some truth to this. Even though my husband continued to insist that this accusation wasn't factual, and as much as I wanted what he was saying to be true, I knew better.

Not knowing exactly what to do, we met with our pastor and first lady. As we discussed the situation, we were encouraged to fast and pray. But because of the tension, we weren't successful in the advice given to us. Early Saturday morning, we sat down to talk. I had my mind made up that this would be my last and final attempt asking him to be honest with me. A part of me hoped he would feel some level of conviction and confess. I asked for the last time, and again he denied it. As I began to look through the emails on his phone, I hadn't initially discovered anything. However, as I opened his sent inbox, I found several messages between him and the girl. The emails confirmed that there had been something going on between them, but still nothing concrete. According to their emails, my husband had been avoiding her by not returning her calls. This resulted in her threatening to contact me if he didn't call her. As he sat there with the look of embarrassment and guilt on his face, he confessed.

Devastated, livid, hurt, angry, disappointed, and over-whelmed; so many emotions consumed me all at once and I could no longer hold it together. All that ran through my mind was how great of a wife I had been to him, how I put up with so much from him and his family, and how I stuck by his side believing in him and believing that someday he would change. Even through the hurt and pain I had already endured within this marriage, it wasn't enough to keep him from causing me more pain. Instead of him apologizing and showing some level of resentment, he was speechless. As my emotions heightened and being overcome by such a great level of hurt and devastation, I physically lashed out. As he restrained me, a glimpse of my childhood appeared before me and I hastily did something that would change our lives forever. I dialed 911.

CHAPTER FOURTEEN

Through The Fire

> When you go through deep waters, I will be with
> you. When you go through rivers of difficulty, you
> will not drown. When you walk through the fire of
> oppression, you will not be burned up; the flames will
> not consume you.
>
> ~Isaiah 43:2~

Almost everyone has encountered situations that have made them feel like giving up. In these times, it's easy to believe that because things are so bad, you could never move ahead and be able to live a meaningful life. Well, this is where I was. I had suffered so much, and all in such a short period of time: the drama, hurt, pain, unwise choices, scrutiny, guilt, judgement, and attacks from the enemy. I felt as though things were never going to get any better. In times where I would have normally had my life mapped out, I didn't know what to do or even what the next steps were for me. My whole world had fallen apart in a blink of an eye. There are times we react to certain situations solely based off emotion, not realizing that reaction has the capability of impacting our lives forever. It had been several days since the incident, and because my husband wasn't present to give his side of the story, he was required for questioning. Ironically, upon being pulled over for a traffic violation, he was met with the opportunity to give his account of the incident. Once he was questioned, it instantly went public. It was all throughout the media. The media is known to embellish the truth, therefore they twisted what occurred for the sake of producing a good story. My life was already a mess, but now it had become a whirlwind.

Almost immediately I started to receive unwanted phone calls. These phone calls occurred during various hours of the night, and because the person initially failed to call anonymously, the number appeared. Not to my surprise, it was my husband's father. I had asked this man over and over to refrain from contacting me, yet he continued. Days later, the phone calls that once consisted of a person breathing and making noises into the phone, turned into threats from a woman. Later down the line, I learned it was my husband's sister. I also learned her father encouraged the call. I couldn't say I was surprised, because this sort of behavior was typical of him. Although I should've been upset with my husband's sister, I wasn't. She didn't know any better and was only doing what she was told to do. Therefore, I overlooked it.

My husband and I were at a crossroads, and it was mainly because of the infidelity. However, his unfaithfulness quickly diminished, and the attention shifted to him being questioned by the police. Suddenly, the adultery held very little importance. Him being publicly scrutinized was more important than him dishonoring a covenant ordained by God. This is a mere reflection of the type of world we live in. There aren't many people who truly honor and respect the institution of marriage. For instance, my husband's father was thrilled that our marriage was on the rocks. He was finally getting what he wanted: our marriage to fail. My husband knew without a shadow of a doubt that his actions is what placed us in this predicament, yet his pride along with bias and un-Godly advice he was receiving, resulted in him disregarding the infidelity. Although my husband was totally innocent in that he has never hit me, this wasn't the case regarding him being unfaithful in his marriage. Nonetheless, he suddenly forgot about what he had done, and the focus was on what I had done.

Did I plan for our situation to go public? Of course not. Quite frankly, if my husband wasn't a well-known politician, the situation wouldn't have received the attention it did. Every couple have their share of arguments and those arguments sometime escalate. Normally, people wouldn't hear of these occurrences; but because of my husband's political status, they did. As hurt and angry as I was, my intent would never be to cause my husband any sort of trouble, legally or career related. This situation was nothing more than a woman reacting out of emotion after having her entire world turned upside down. The last thing on my mind was devising a plan to take my husband down. He's my husband and the father of my child, therefore, what happens to him ultimately affects our daughter as well as myself.

I wasn't enjoying any of the events that had taken place. I was hurting because of the infidelity, and on top of that, I was faced with gossip and judgement. Having to face my issues publicly, was difficult. But I couldn't allow it to consume me. Although most women wouldn't probably admit it, there are women who would have reacted entirely worse than I did if they were in my shoes. Amid the judgement and criticism, I held my head high and stood my ground. No one was walking in my shoes, they didn't know what I was dealing with and how I was feeling. People are quick to say what they would've done if they were in a situation, but when it happens to them, their whole point of view shifts. The bottom line is: I reacted out of emotion, and I accept my mistake as a learning and growing experience.

Even though I was furious with my husband, it bothered me knowing he was being publicly labeled as something he wasn't. It also bothered me to see the negative impact of my actions. It's something how one impulsive reaction can drastically change your life forever. Although myself and people close to us knew the things said about my husband in the media wasn't true, I was still troubled by it. Nonetheless, I had to get to a place where I could no longer worry myself with things I had no control over. My marriage had reached a point of destruction and I needed to focus on what the next chapter would be for me.

Although there were a few of my husband's relatives who didn't care much for me, there were also some I had rapport with. Shortly after the incident, I reached out to an aunt of his. In the past, she and I have had conversations regarding how I had been treated and she always seemed to be in support of my marriage. I felt as though she and I had built a genuine relationship, so I contacted her. When I called her, I initially thought she was going to express compassion toward what I was going through as she had done in the past. However, she instantly began saying that she felt sorry for the girl my husband cheated on me with. She shared with me that the girl called her crying and expressing how much she loved my husband. I couldn't fathom what I was hearing! Outside of being completely caught off guard regarding her connection to this girl, I also found it difficult to understand how someone could be so inconsiderate of another person's feelings. For her to think it was okay to say something so insensitive to a wife who had just learned of her husband's infidelity, truly revealed her character. She also stated in our conversation that she advised my husband to get his own place to live. What I was hearing was far beyond appalling. I totally didn't expect to hear anything remotely like this when I decided to contact her. To advise a man who has committed adultery to leave his wife, is blatantly disrespectful and out of place. I was completely blindsided. This was a woman I believed truly cared for me. Not only was it obvious she had a relationship with this girl, it was also clear she didn't support my marriage the way she led me to believe. She showed more compassion for a side chick than she did a wife. It took some time for me to put things into perspective, but once I did I realized I wasn't having a conversation with a woman of God, a married woman, or even a woman of compassion. This situation revealed she lacked respect and honor for marriage. Therefore, I couldn't expect anything more than what she gave. When experiencing obstacles in life, it's important to be mindful of who we turn to for support. There's a saying, "When someone shows you who they are, believe them." I learned a valuable lesson, which is to use wisdom regarding who you share your business with and solicit advice from. Everyone isn't going to be in your corner and support you the way you would expect them to. Unfortunately, it took me learning the hard the way, but I sure did learn.

Hurt is a natural reaction when involving betrayal, and anger usually accompanies it. These emotions can sometimes cause a person to react in a way they normally wouldn't. Speaking for myself, there was a time shortly after learning of my husband's infidelity where I came face to face with his mistress. Although the incident isn't something I'm proud of, I accept I wasn't being led by the spirit; and therefore, I acted out of character. My behavior in that moment didn't define me as a person, but it has helped me to understand how important it is to have control of your emotions.

I was mentally and emotionally overwhelmed. The anguish and fear of what the future held consumed me. I didn't know what to do. All I knew was that I didn't want to continue being married to a cheater, so what did I do? I sought legal counsel. As I sat with the attorney, I couldn't believe the place my life had come to. Every memory of my marriage replayed vividly in my mind; the good and the bad. Was I about to make the right choice in moving forward with divorce, was I making a hasty decision, and was it really what God wanted me to do? I was lost, and all hope had departed from me. I felt abandoned and all alone. While in this state of desolation, I began to understand God's purpose for everything I had been going through. We often give credit to the enemy and blame him for the storms we encounter, but the reality is there's nothing Satan can do that God doesn't allow. Satan doesn't have free reign over our lives. For example, in the story of Job, the devil received direct permission from God to attack Job. Job lost everything important to him, yet he remained faithful to God. God's sovereignty during a time of great suffering was illustrated in this story. Not only was this story an illustration of how sovereign God is, God's faithfulness was also displayed. Although God allowed Job to be stripped of everything he had, He gave him back twice as much (see Job 1:8-12, 42:10-17). God is so amazing that when He allows us to experience difficult times, He brings us out even better than what we were before. So often we want to hold onto what we have and what's familiar and comfortable for us; but just like Job, it's always best to trust and remain faithful to God. He loves us more than we could ever love ourselves and therefore, what He has for us totally outweighs any plans we have for ourselves.

God allows us to go through the fire, so He can make us better. So often we focus on the surface of our situation that we miss the deeper purpose. We experience suffering for many different reasons. It may be the result of what we have done and most often, what has been done to us. Whether it is the result of our own actions or the actions of someone else, our sufferings have the capability of bringing about a range of emotions, with a common one being guilt. We blame ourselves and play the "If" game. "If I had not made that decision, then this would have never happened." This mindset does nothing more than keep us stagnant, and this is exactly where Satan wants us. It's a stronghold that keeps us chained to the past, unable to move beyond what has happened. What I've learned is regardless if we are guilty or not, the feeling of guilt speaks to us so consistently that it becomes our reality. The inability to move forward allows our past to define and consume us with little to no hope of a productive future. This isn't living, nor is it God designed. This type of living has Satan written all over it. His goal is to kill, steal and destroy. I had one of two choices: be overcome by my situation or overcome my situation. I decided I would begin living the life God had for me! I was no longer going to give Satan authority over my life, nor was I going to be controlled by my past. I no longer wanted to live my life according to what happened, what should have happened, and even what people thought of me. No one truly knew what I was dealing with, but God; and ultimately, all that matters is what He thinks.

CHAPTER FIFTEEN

The Great Tribulation

Blessed is the man who remains steadfast under trial,
for when he has stood the test he will receive the
crown of life, which God has promised to those who
love him.

~James 1:12 ESV~

I've always believed our trials come to make us strong. Well, I was more convinced now than ever that this storm was designed to do just that. I was going through; I mean really going through. There's no way of all the mess I was dealing with, that it was all going to be in vain. There was a purpose for it all, there had to be. God loved me too much. It says in His word, that He will never leave me nor forsake me (see Deuteronomy 31:6, NIV). I believed what His word said and held onto it, expecting one day I'd receive my breakthrough.

For a long time, I would wonder; "Why me?" But eventually God revealed to me, "Why not?" Luke 22:42 says, "Father, if thou be willing, remove this cup from me: nevertheless, not my will, but thine, be done." When we start realizing our lives are not our own; but God's, it is then when we will begin to understand that it's about what He wants for us, not what we want for ourselves. It's important to trust Him through our trials, no matter what they look or feel like. I truly believe when there's an anointing on your life, there are going to be many trials and tribulations we will encounter. I'm not referring to the typical trials and tribulations we of life; I'm talking about the type of storms that will knock you down and have you wondering if it's even possible to get back up. In these times, you realize how faithful and true God really is; I know I did. Truth of the matter is: we will not experience any pain that Jesus hasn't already known. Nothing can even come close to all He endured for us to be saved. Death by crucifixion is the most painful experience I can imagine and Jesus suffering on the cross is far more unbearable than what any of us has had to experience here on Earth. Because Jesus suffered, we too will experience suffering. We are not exempt from facing trials, we aren't even promised a life without tests, but we are promised a God who will walk beside us in those difficult times. Psalm 34:19 (KJV) says, "Many are the afflictions of the righteous: but the LORD delivereth him out of them all." What's so awesome about God is that He knows what we will go through before we go through it. Because He knows, He gives us strength to weather the storm and equips us with what we need in the most brutal seasons of our human experience.

When we are smack dead in the middle of a trial, the last thing we think is that it's temporary. But it's true; our trials are only temporary, but the word of God is embedded in us forever as a tool to help us along the way. As difficult as my trial was, I didn't give up, even in moments I wanted to. Depression, stress, worry, unhappiness and feelings of defeat tried to overcome me. If I had allowed it to, it would have ultimately meant Satan would win, and I wasn't going to let that happen. I had no choice but to find joy within all the junk I was dealing with, junk that was thrown at me, junk I created, and even the junk I allowed. It wasn't easy. Some days were good and other days were not so good. The moment I thought things were getting better, I was reminded they weren't. I had no idea what God was doing. I was frustrated, and ready for a change to take place, but it wasn't happening fast enough. I felt stuck and as if my life was at a standstill. In hindsight, I was exactly where God wanted me.

God transforms us through our trials. A transition is an in-between time, a move from something familiar to unfamiliar, a move from the way things once were to the way they are going to be, and a move from the old to the new. This process may take longer for some, but the results will always be the same; which is becoming a new person. You will not be the same, you won't see things the same, you won't even act the same, you will be all around different. The Bible says, "Consider it pure joy, my brothers and sisters, whenever you face trials of many kinds, because you know that the testing of your faith produces perseverance. Let perseverance finish its work so that you may be mature and complete, not lacking anything," (James 1:2-4, NIV). Every trial I've faced was specifically designed for me. It wasn't by error or default. God ordained it. Anyone else, perhaps, couldn't have handled it. It was handcrafted just for me. My story is my story, just like the next person's story is theirs. Often, there's resistance in difficult times. However, trials aren't curses, they are gifts. If we view it from the standpoint of God shaping and molding us, transforming us, preparing us for something better and ultimately placing us in a position where we are closer to reaching our destiny, maybe we would be more understanding and embracing of the trials we face. Patience is the key in times like this. If you choose to take matters into your own hands like I have done many times, you are interfering in God's business and making matters worse. God has a plan for our lives and we must be patient enough to trust Him.

As much as I appeared to be handling things well, the truth is I initially wanted badly for my storm to pass. It didn't feel good and I wanted desperately for it to be over. It's natural to want to overcome our trials as quickly as possible. But if we do, we miss out on the lesson. Since it didn't seem as though my storm was going to end anytime soon, my prayer was for God to sustain me through it. Just like James said, whenever we face trials of all sorts, we are to count them as pure joy. The Bible didn't say, "sometimes," it said "whenever." It didn't even say, "some trials," it said, "trials of all sorts." Counting our trials as pure joy simply means to rejoice in the trials with a spirit of expectation that God will do what He said; and that's bring you out. Trials have a way of stripping away everything until we're left staring at the remaining delicate pieces of our lives, not knowing exactly what to do with them. As for me, I was a good person, I loved the Lord, worked hard, tried to do right, prayed, attended church and helped others, yet it didn't stop this trial from occurring. I didn't understand why at first, but it was through this tribulation that God began to reveal it. We encounter trials to test our faith. We can either resist it or accept it. I chose to accept it, for I knew it meant I was closer to God and closer to reaching my purpose in Him. God was elevating me. I was being developed, and through this development, everything I encountered was necessary for me to become exactly who God created me to be. Romans 8:18 says, "Yet what we suffer now is nothing compared to the glory he will reveal to us later." God had great things in store for me, I just needed to trust Him. Even though it didn't look good or feel good, I stood on the promises of God and believed, this too shall pass.

CHAPTER SIXTEEN

Shame on Them

So now there is no condemnation for those who belong to Christ Jesus.

~ Romans 8:1 ~

"**Y**ou don't know my story, you don't know the things that I've come through; you cannot imagine the pain and trials I've had to endure." These are the lyrics of one of my favorite gospel songs by John P. Kee, Life and Favor. There's truth behind these words. People are quick to speak on someone's situation without having a clue as to what that person has had to endure. It's even more devastating when judgement finds its way amongst people you're close to. Those relationships you knew without a shadow of a doubt would be a support in a time you needed it most, turned out to be the total opposite. People judge your situation based off what they feel you should have or shouldn't have done. God's word says, "Do not judge others, and you will not be judged. Do not condemn others, or it will all come back against you. Forgive others, and you will be forgiven," (Luke 6:37). We can be so insensitive and critical toward others and their situations, knowing this is the last thing we want to receive if we were in their shoes. Instead of encouraging and uplifting one another in prayer, we judge and gossip. Reality is, we don't have the right to judge, this job solely belongs to God. "God alone, who gave the law, is the Judge. He alone has the power to save or to destroy. So, what right do you have to judge your neighbor?" (James 4:12). I had to keep reminding myself, man doesn't have a heaven or hell to put me in. Therefore, I shouldn't allow what people thought of me and said about me affect me. Although this is true, it wasn't that simple.

My life at the time was a disaster, my marriage had fallen apart, and my personal life was on display. If you say you've never cared just a little bit about what someone has said or thought about you, then I tip my hat off to you. On the other hand, most people have cared about the opinions of others at some point within their lifetime. It's called being human. This was an area I once struggled with. Although I didn't like this about myself, it was my reality. In fact, I wanted badly to change it. I believed I cared too much in times I shouldn't have. I realized there was an underlying reason for this. Aside from being a private person and dreading the idea of my personal business being laid out on a platter, I realized I was projecting my own fears and self-judgment onto other people. As I thought about it, it made sense; I was judging myself for some of the same things people were judging me for.

The more I tried to brush it off, the more I cared. I recall going in public for the first time after the incident occurred between me and my husband. I had never felt so uncomfortable and out of place in my life, but I knew I would eventually have to face reality. No one brought up the incident, but because of my own feelings of regret and guilt, I felt they were thinking it. Despite how I felt, I held my head high and kept a smile on my face. I was going through hell, and the last thing I wanted was to look like it. I refused to give anyone something more to talk about. If they were going to talk about anything, it was going to be "how I didn't look like what I was going through". It wasn't because of anything I had done. It wasn't the makeup, my hairstyle or even the clothes I wore, it was all God. He sustained me. Just like God brought Shadrach, Meshach, and Abednego out of the fiery furnace untouched, without a trace that they had ever been there; God covered me in the same way (see Daniel 3). Even though the enemy came in like a flood, he still couldn't destroy me. God kept me and didn't allow me to be consumed by the fire.

Allowing the opinions and gossip of others to affect me was preventing me from growing. I finally accepted that it's impossible change anyone's opinion and I shouldn't be concerned with it anyway. There's an old saying, "Sticks and stones may break my bones, but words will never hurt me." I'm sure many of us were told this when we were younger. However, the truth is, words do hurt. "The words of the reckless pierce like swords, but the tongue of the wise brings healing," (Proverbs

12:18, NIV). We must be mindful of the things we allow to come out of our mouths, it has the capability of damaging a person's spirit. When it's all said and done, those who use other people's downfalls maliciously or as an opportunity for gossip, will have to answer to God for it. We must start being the light we want to receive and treating people the way we want to be treated. Therefore, despite how people spoke negatively about me and my situation, I remained positive. Their actions didn't stop anything; I was growing spiritually, becoming a better person, and receiving what God had for me.

Caring about things I had no control of didn't add any value to my life. In fact, it was draining and stressful. Because of fear and embarrassment, we sometimes allow what others say and think of us keep us from living our best lives. People had a lot to say and because I allowed it to bother me, I wasn't living the life God intended, I was living to please them. I realized that people are always going to have something to say. You can't control it, nor can you change it; there's absolutely nothing you can do about it. Majority of those who are doing the gossiping and judging, don't know you or your situation anyway. Therefore, what they say doesn't matter. The only opinion that truly matters is God's and your own.

While adapting to no longer worrying about those things that had no precedence over my life, I was also empowered to stop being so critical and judgmental of myself. I'm not perfect, I have made many mistakes. I'm finally okay in knowing my mistakes are not a reflection of who I am as a person, but instead are learning opportunities. When someone judges you, it doesn't define who you are; it defines who they are. Even with all the gossip, ridicule, persecution, and judgment, God favored me. He did not allow me to be consumed by people's thoughts and opinions of me. In fact, He gave me the boldness to stand firm in my truth. Although it was a process getting to the place I am today, I'm glad I'm no longer concerned and bothered by those things. I've grown in many ways. I've learned to let whoever think whatever; they're going to do it anyway. It's easy to lose yourself in trying to please those around you. The truth is, it's impossible to please God and man at the same time. I have gained wisdom in not letting people's judgment, criticism, gossip, and opinions affect me. I've also learned not to be so hard on myself. I'm going to make mistakes, but the great part is that I serve a God who's able to turn my mistakes into masterpieces. Because of Him, I am confident in who I am. I am unshakeable, and I walk confidently in my truth.

CHAPTER SEVENTEEN

From Shame to Gain

As Scripture says, "Anyone who believes in him will never be put to shame."

~Romans 10:11 NIV~

Shame can cause us to blame ourselves for things we didn't do. I honored my marriage, I didn't cheat, I didn't lie, I was good to my husband, but I was ashamed. I'll tell you why... when something negatively happens in our lives, especially at the hand of someone we love, no matter how devastating it may be, we still choose to see the good in that person. Out of love, we may even take on the burdens of their wrongdoings. As angry as I was at my husband for all he had done, when the dust settled and the anger somewhat subsided, I still loved him. I knew aside from the various mistakes he made, he was a good person. However, aside from him being a good person, I was a great wife and I didn't deserve to be mistreated. I defended my husband when he wasn't doing the same for me and had his back like no else did; all I got in return was unfaithfulness, lies, and deceit. Overwhelmed with shame, I felt like a fool. The embarrassment was more than I could bear.

It's a terrible feeling being the last to know something… especially regarding your spouse. In marriage, husbands and wives should be the go to people for one another. They should always be aware of what the other has going on. No one should ever be able to tell you anything about your spouse that you already don't know. It's a partnership; however, this wasn't the case for my marriage. I was in the dark about everything. It seemed like other people knew how my husband felt, what he was doing, and who he was doing it with, except for me. A husband should never put his wife in a situation where she's being looked at by others like, "if she only knew." A wife deserves her husband's utmost respect and honor. Her name, character, and dignity should be uplifted by her husband at all times. The cheating alone was devastating enough, but people knowing of it when I didn't; was a different level of disrespect.

Aside from the infidelity, pretty much everyone had heard about the incident; it was public news. I had never received so many phone calls and texts at one time. Although most people reached out with a genuine concern, there were those who used the opportunity to pry. As bad as things were, I tried my best not to lose focus. My daughter depended on me and deserved my full attention. Being her mommy didn't end because a storm decided to come my way. I had to keep pushing, I couldn't give up. But I couldn't do it on my own, God picked me up, held me in His arms and gave me the strength I needed to stand. Although it wasn't coming quick enough, I knew eventually things would blow over and people would move on to the next piece of gossip. Nevertheless, I was ready for it all to be over.

I couldn't believe all I had gone through. I had only been married three years, and I had experienced hell and high water. I carried the burden of regret and shame for so long. It was mentally destroying me. No matter how we try to rewrite or change the past, it's impossible to do so. The reality was I chose to marry my husband, and therefore I had to accept everything that came with it, the good and even the bad. Husbands and wives are representatives for one another. While I felt I had honored and represented him properly, he hadn't done the same for me, and it was embarrassing. I eventually acknowledged that I could no longer allow myself to be troubled by what he wasn't doing. I had been a great wife and I wasn't going to continue to carry the burden as if I hadn't.

I gained so much wisdom from what I was going through. Even though it was uncomfortable, sometimes discomfort is necessary for growth to occur. I knew I was on a journey predestined by God. I was growing and trusting in Him more than I had ever before. This was only the beginning. I had a long way to go, but I was beginning to feel empowered and hopeful about what the future had in store. As I embraced this chapter in my life, I realized God allowed everything to occur for a greater purpose. It wasn't to embarrass me, it wasn't to humiliate me…it was to elevate me. There was no room for shame in my life. I made the decision to be proud of my story, for it's a part of who I am. Although there were many bumps along the way, it ultimately allowed me to develop a closer relationship with God.

In reflecting on the events that transpired within my marriage, I have truly grown to accept God's will for my life, even the painful parts. God loves me and the love He has for me didn't change because of my trials or mistakes. I now realize that I have nothing to be ashamed of. Everyone has a story that consists of mistakes, failures, and hardships. They are there to help us grow and become who we are destined to be. I've learned life lessons that I might not have learned had it not been for what I had gone through. I am wiser. I have the courage to share my story and hopefully inspire someone who has gone through something similar. Shame no longer resides here. I embrace where I have been, just as much as where I am headed.

CHAPTER EIGHTEEN

NO Weapon Formed Against Me Shall Prosper

*No weapon that is formed against thee shall prosper;
and every tongue that shall rise against thee in
judgment thou shalt condemn. This is the heritage of
the servants of the LORD, and their righteousness is of
me, saith the LORD.*

~Isaiah 54:17 (KJV)~

The enemy comes to kill, steal, and destroy…but that's only if you let him. Throughout my storm, God had been speaking to me regarding the scripture "no weapon formed against you shall prosper." Every time the enemy threw something my way, this scripture was there as a reminder that he would not win. However, I must be honest in saying there were moments where I felt defeated. The attacks were one after the other. Satan was stopping at nothing to take me out. I was going through hell, yet it didn't stop me from giving God praise. I was in the fight of my life and had come too far to lose.

Once people became aware of there being trouble in my marriage, the gossip escalated. Suddenly people who had no reason to be concerned with what was going on in my life, took an interest. It's true that people gravitate to any sort of gossip just for the sake of having something to talk about. Just about every time I turned around, people were either commenting on my marriage or approaching me with information regarding things they had heard. Although my marriage was being publicly dissected, I was trying to deal as best I could with it. From determining how I wanted to move forward in my marriage, to being constantly reminded of my husband's indiscretions, I couldn't escape. I was right where Satan wanted me: depressed, angry, and worried.

For us to really see the will of God, we must sometimes remove ourselves from outside influences. It's imperative before making decisions, to first consult with God. I wanted to do what God wanted me to do, but I just didn't know exactly what that consisted of. I was constantly being reminded of my husband's infidelity and it was making my decision to dissolve the marriage easy. Maybe this was God leading me or perhaps it was Satan's way of distracting me; I didn't know. I recall having a conversation with my First Lady. In that conversation, she told me I needed to be mindful of the intentions of people. She said when God wants you to know something it's not going to be delivered in a malicious or messy way; God doesn't operate this way. In this moment, I had to consider who God was. He's love, peace, patience, kindness, all things good, and all things wonderful. He is never attached to anything evil, and therefore after reflecting on the advice I received, I had clarity. God will make it crystal clear as to what He wants us to do, and He doesn't need assistance in doing this. Therefore, I began to ignore those individuals who were gossiping, bringing me information and speaking negatively about my marriage. I trusted that whatever God wanted me to do; whether it being divorce or to fight for my marriage, it would be revealed in due season. Once I began to block all outside influences and stopped engaging in damaging conversation, those things no longer had power over me. Hebrews 10:36 says, "Patient endurance is what you need now, so that you will continue to do God's will. Then you will receive all that he has promised." My mind was on God and pleasing Him. In doing this, I gained wisdom, patience, and clarity.

Satan tried everything. He attacked me through my marriage, family, friendships, job, and even my mind. There's something special about being a child of God and knowing that you are never alone, that He's always by your side even in times when it doesn't seem like it. No weapon the enemy formed against me, prospered. His plan did not work; he could not steal my joy. God blocked every plan the enemy had for me. I could have lost my mind, but God kept me. I could have given up, but God wouldn't let me. I could have even avenged those who hurt me, but God said no. God covered me, and I'm a living testament that no matter what you go through and how bad it is, God has you. He loves His children so much not to let us fail. I know from experience that your enemies can't do anything with you when God is on your side. Ephesians 6:11 (NIV) says, "Put on the full armor of God, so that you can take your stand against the devil's schemes." The moment I realized the battles I was facing weren't carnal, but spiritual, and started fighting in the spirit is when those devils started to flee. So often we look at things for what they appear to be and not for what they really are. I was in a spiritual war and had I continued to fight it in the physical, I would have been defeated, but God said, "Not my child."

My past had a strong hold on me. I couldn't imagine ever getting to a place of peace. Even though I was taking one step at a time, it seemed like with every step I was getting pulled backwards. I knew holding on to the past was causing more harm than good; it was hindering my growth and happiness. I didn't want to continue living in the past; I wanted to heal from all the pain I had experienced. I made the decision to stop dwelling on what happened and instead, I shifted my focus to my future. Luke 9:62 says, "No one who puts his hands to the plow and looks back is fit for the kingdom of God." The past is called the past for a reason, and it should be left where it is, in the past. There's no way to change it; it can't be rewritten, nor do we get a do-over. We learn from it and move forward.

In deciding to not look back, the enemy attempted another attack. I was yet again faced with an unexpected situation and placed in a position I never thought I would have to be in: filing for an order of protection. I had never been in a situation or felt the need to seek legal protection from anyone ever in my life, but after being constantly threatened, harassed, and slandered by my husband's father, I knew I had to do something. This wasn't normal behavior, yet it was enough for me to wonder if he would ever stop. I needed to take his behavior seriously. I needed to protect myself. His threats could no longer be ignored. After attending multiple court hearings all due to him either avoiding being served, his lack of attendance, and even him being dishonest with the courts saying he's a police officer in an effort of getting the order denied, I was mentally drained. I went back and forth regarding should I continue to pursue the order and was any of this even worth it? Should I forget about it and hope that one day he'll stop bothering me? I wasn't sure if I had the energy and strength to move forward, but just when I was about to give up, the restraining order was granted.

I'll never forget how I felt walking out of the courtroom, the anxiety I had been carrying for so long had diminished. All I endured from this man, God truly moved on my behalf; I didn't have to do anything but trust Him. I didn't have to fight back or say a word; God fought for me. Scripture says, "The Lord will fight for you; you need only to be still," (Exodus 14:14, NIV). God fought my battle and it's because of Him that the enemy didn't triumph over me. I experienced a calmness I hadn't felt in a long time. I no longer had to worry about my safety or my peace of mind. I could finally begin to focus on myself and receiving healing. I am not bitter or angry, for now I understand that my husband's father served a purpose in me reaching my destiny. Without the negative, the positive wouldn't exist. We must go through the bad to get to the good. He was only a vessel being used by the enemy in attempting to destroy and derail me from reaching my destiny. Therefore, my issue isn't with him, it's with Satan. I discovered peace in the following scripture, "He who dwells in the shelter of the Most High will abide in the shadow of the Almighty. I will say to the Lord, "My refuge and my fortress, my God, in whom I trust." For He will deliver you from the snare of the fowler and from the deadly pestilence. He will cover you with His pinions, and under His wings you will find refuge; His faithfulness is a shield and buckler. You will not fear the terror of the night, nor the arrow that flies by day, nor the pestilence that stalks in darkness, nor the destruction that wastes at noonday. A thousand may fall at your side, ten thousand at your right hand, but it will not come near you. You will only look with your eyes and see the recompense of the wicked. Because you have made the Lord your dwelling place----the Most High, who is my refuge----no evil shall be allowed to befall you, no plague come near your tent. For He will command His angels concerning you to guard you in all your ways. On their hands they will bear you up, lest you strike your foot against stone. You will tread on the lion and the serpent you will trample underfoot. Because he holds fast to me in love, I will deliver him; I will protect him, because he knows my name. When he calls to me, I will answer him; I will be with him in trouble; I will rescue him and honor him. With long life, I will satisfy him and show him my salvation," (Psalms 91:1-16, ESV). God saved me from the hand of the enemy. I am at peace.

CHAPTER NINETEEN

Savannah Sunshine

*When a woman is giving birth, she has sorrow
because her hour has come, but when she has delivered
the baby, she no longer remembers the anguish, for joy
that a human being has been born into the world.*
~John 16:21 ESV~

I didn't have what some women would refer to as, "the best pregnancy." Make no mistake, I was extremely excited about becoming a mother, but there were so many stressors in my life at the time. Nonetheless, I decided to focus on the joy of becoming a mother and not my circumstances. I enjoyed carrying my child, experiencing her growing and feeling her move inside of me, was amazing. What I didn't like is that the most joyous time in my life was being shared with the most stressful time in my life. My marriage was in turmoil, I wasn't in a happy place. I was overwhelmed. Regardless of how challenging things were, I refused to let it take from the happiness of me becoming a mother. In such a tumultuous time in my life, the only peace I had is what I found through my unborn child. I hadn't even met her yet, and she made me smile. Savannah was my happy place.

I've always been told the love between a mother and child is indescribable. After experiencing it for myself, I couldn't agree more. Loving someone so deeply and profoundly is such a blessing. "Children are a gift from the LORD; they are a reward from him," (Psalm 127:3). There is nothing more amazing than what's experienced through childbirth; twenty-one and a half hours of labor, resulting in an emergency Cesarean, my baby girl was born. She was perfect in every way imaginable, a special blessing from God. My whole world instantly changed. She brought out the best in me, helping me to become a better version of myself. I was amazed at the woman I was becoming. Being her mother has brought meaning to my life, and with each day comes new joy. I have something to look forward to and someone in this world to love me unconditionally. Because of her, I didn't give up at times I wanted to. She was exactly what I needed in a time I needed it most. We've been taught that when we have children, we are to care for them, provide for them, and nurture them. It's amazing how our children can end up helping us just as much as we help them. I don't think I would've had the strength to fight through the hard times if it wasn't for God blessing me with my daughter. Because of her, I possessed strength that surpassed my comprehension and had a reason to push through this thing called life.

We've all heard that children can sense when there's something wrong. Well, I found this to be true. It was always my priority to never allow my daughter to see me cry or upset. I didn't want to burden her with my emotions, especially at such a young age. I wanted her to experience an unmeasurable amount of happiness no matter what was going on around her. It was my goal to prevent my issues from impacting her. But as much I tried to shield her from it, she could sense something was wrong. I recall one day my one-year-old daughter hugged me and patted my back saying, "Mommy, you're the best." In complete shock and overwhelmed with joy, tears slowly rolled down my cheeks as I tightly hugged my baby girl. This is a perfect example of grace and unconditional love. If we learn anything from our children, it's love. Emotionally, I was at rock bottom and those little words spoken from my one-year-old reminded me of God's love. I truly believe God speaks to us through our children. He knew exactly what I was feeling and going through and this was His way of reminding me that I wasn't alone. In our weakest most detrimental moments, God embraces us; His grace and love covers us.

When it comes to motherhood, everything else is secondary. My world at the time consisted of major chaos, drama and dysfunction. It was not a healthy environment for an adult, let alone a child. Although I was surrounded by complete confusion, it was important for me to create a peaceful and positive atmosphere for my child. Growing up in dysfunction, I knew exactly what it looked like and I even knew the impact it could potentially have on a child. For this reason alone, I chose to show my daughter something different than what I experienced. Raising her in an environment that is God-filled, love-filled, and peace-filled is and will forever be my priority.

Motherhood is a blessing and responsibility I deeply cherish. As mothers, we are responsible for laying the foundation for the type of individuals our children will become. Values, morals, and integrity are all important factors that play a dynamic role in a child's future, and it starts with us. We must be the example we want to see in them. Our children are watching us, even when we may not realize it. My daughter is my mini me. At various times, I've noticed her mimicking me. Although it's a great feeling to have someone look up to you, it's also important to be cognizant of the things we say and do. As women, we are the first example and influence our daughters will have of how a woman should carry and respect herself. It's up to us to teach them how young ladies should act. One of the best ways in doing this is being a woman of God. It's my priority to instill in her at an early age who God is. As I said before, it starts with us. We cannot teach what we don't possess. For example, if my daughter doesn't see me living a lifestyle aligned in the word of God, then how can I expect for her to have a relationship with Him. Our children are motivated in knowing God for themselves through the relationship they see we have with Him. Quite honestly, my desire for my daughter to know God, has helped me in becoming closer to God. Proverbs 22:6 KJV says, "Train up a child in the way he should go: and when he is old, he will not depart from it." I trust that if my daughter happens to get off track at some point throughout her life, those same values and morals I instill in her will always be there to lead her back to God. God has entrusted me with the responsibility of being her mother. I am thankful, I am humbled, and it is a commitment I take very seriously.

Savannah is a happy child, and this brings me an excessive amount of joy. Seeing her smile is one of life's greatest pleasures. She is full of life and a total delight to be around. She has the best personality, more than what I could have ever asked for. At the tender age of two, there isn't a day that goes by that this little girl doesn't make me wonder if she's really two. From her intellect to her sassiness, great sense of humor, vivaciousness, fearlessness, loving and compassionate personality; she is absolutely amazing. Among all the great qualities she possesses, her love and reverence for God at such a young age takes the cake. It is simply remarkable when your two-year-old bows her head to say grace, when she joins in for family prayer and sometimes leads the prayer, and even during church when she claps and raises her hands saying Hallelujah. The spirit of God inevitably dwells within my child and I couldn't be more overjoyed. I thank God for blessing me with such an incredible daughter. Her light shines so bright, bright enough that is has lightened my darkest days. It's amazing how something so small has been able to brighten up my entire world. God used my daughter to keep me. Lord knows if it wasn't for her, I probably would've given up. Her dependence on me sustained me, strengthened me, and gave me hope when life seemed impossible. Our connection and bond is impeccable, and something I will always be thankful for. These past few years of being her mother have taught me so much and have also brought me an immense amount of joy, motivation, inspiration, and unconditional love. I am greatly honored for her to call me Mommy. My life is forever changed. Motherhood has become my greatest achievement and it's all because of God's little blessing: Savannah.

CHAPTER TWENTY

Faith Walk

For we walk by faith, not by sight.
~2 Corinthians 5:7 (ESV)~

Have you ever gone through a tough time and all you did was worry, stress, and doubt that it would get any better? If so, what happened once things turned out to be okay, did you regret your reaction? How would it be if when we face trials, instead of worrying, we immediately trust that God will work it out? This would certainly be pleasing to God. However, things are not always this easy. For some, it takes a variety of experiences to truly understand the importance of trusting God and knowing tough times strengthens faith. For instance, every time I've gone through something, my initial reaction always consisted of me worrying. However, after things ended up working out for my good; which they always did, it was then that I began to feel guilty for doubting God in the first place. All the unnecessary energy and time spent stressing over the situation could have been avoided if I understood what it meant to truly trust God.

What I've learned is that Satan will try everything he can to destroy our faith by making us believe God doesn't care for us. However, we must be reminded of the scripture that says, "casting all your cares [all your anxieties, all your worries, and all your concerns, once and for all] on Him, for He cares about you [with deepest affection, and watches over you very carefully]" (1 Peter 5:7, AMP). As I grew more in the Lord, my mindset started to change. I began to understand that because God loves me so deeply, He will always take care of me. Therefore, I no longer wanted to respond in a way that reflected me not having faith in Him. Instead of reacting without hope, I wanted my actions to reflect a great level of trust in God.

Trusting God involves believing in Him for everything. The word says, "trust in the Lord with all your heart," (Proverbs 3:5, NIV). It doesn't say "trust in the Lord with some of your heart." This means to fully and completely rely on Him no matter what the circumstances are. My experiences strengthened my faith and I gained so much knowledge and wisdom through my trials. Had it not been for the things I had gone through, I probably would be the same person: doubting, stressing, and worrying about any and everything. "Faith is the substance of things hoped for and the evidence of things not seen," (Hebrews 11:1, KJV). It's believing your situation will change for the better even in times you can't see it getting any better. Faith is about action. Our faith is exercised by us showing hope for something we can't yet see. This is done by believing Jesus exists. By believing He exists, we believe everything about Him. When you truly believe in Christ, you believe that even though you don't understand all things, He does. There isn't a better or more reliable person to place our faith in other than Him. There's nothing we go through that God hasn't already experienced or doesn't understand. Because Jesus overcame the world, He knows exactly how to help us overcome our most difficult times (see John 16:33).

God only allows things to happen to us that he knows we can survive, but quite often we don't want to go through anything. What we must understand is when God takes us through something, it's because He's preparing us for something greater. When there's an anointing on our life there will be obstacles, challenges, difficulties, heartache, pain, sorrow etc. Many times, I found myself in situations I felt were unbearable. It was then I realized, these situations wouldn't have come my way had it not been a part of God's plan for my life. Isaiah 64:8 says, "And yet, O LORD, you are our Father. We are the clay, and you are the potter. We all are formed by your hand." Being spiritually shaped and molded takes patience and perseverance, but what's so great about it, is being handcrafted by God Himself. It was through my faith walk that I learned the importance of what it meant to wait on the Lord. When we truly wait on God, we receive exactly what He promised us. There's no such thing as rushing God, He moves at His own pace and time. Getting on the potter's wheel is one obstacle, but staying there is another. It's one thing to say you trust God, but what happens when a storm comes your way; will you still trust Him? As servants of God, we are to be willing vessels, allowing God to use us however He desires. If we consider the work of a potter, before taking the clay and forming it into an object, they know beforehand exactly what that object is going to become. Well just like a potter, God knows exactly what our purpose would be before we were even born. He has our lives mapped out. So often, we resist what God has for us out of fear of going through some things. But we must experience the bad, so we will appreciate the good. We will never reach our destiny and know our true purpose if we fail to learn the lesson within our hardships.

Quite some time had passed since the incident between my husband and I, and although I wasn't exactly where I wanted to be, I wasn't where I once was. My trust in the Lord was far greater than I imagined it being. I was closer to God and changing more every day. My viewpoint was different, the way I talked was different, my walk was different, and even the company I kept was different. I was changing, and I owed it all to God. Although everything wasn't exactly how I wanted it to be, my faith in God didn't allow me to focus on those things. I was blessed to no longer have the same mindset. Spiritual growth will cause us to react to certain situations differently than how we normally would. Before realizing it, we will no longer be engaging in conversations and relationships that lack substance and are detrimental to our walk with Christ. When you grow in the Lord, you change for the better. Some people will see you in a different light and will be in support of your change, while others won't. The ones who won't, will be looking for any indication of the old you. They won't believe in the change and this is totally okay. Allow your walk to do the talking. You have nothing to prove to man; especially those whose goal is to constantly remind you of the person you used to be and your past mistakes. Let those people think what they choose while you continue to grow. I wasn't the same person and it didn't matter if people believed it or not. I was connected to God in a way I had never been, and I was loving it. The Bible says in Colossians 2:6-7, "And now, just as you accepted Christ Jesus as your Lord, you must continue to follow him. Let your roots grow down into him, and let your lives be built on him. Then your faith will grow strong in the truth you were taught, and you will overflow with thankfulness." I was grateful for everything: the good, the bad, and even the ugly. I believed that no matter what came my way, without a doubt God would be right there just like He had been before.

God receives the glory for every one of my victories. Nothing I've overcome, whether it was in my childhood or adulthood, I take credit for. God gets it all. One day you may be smiling and then the next you may feel like your whole world has fallen apart; this is life. We must embrace the parts that don't always feel good, they are placed there for a reason. Life can sometimes hurt and leave you feeling heartbroken, disappointed and betrayed among so many other things, but it's all a part of God's plan in making you. You can either allow it to kill you or you can do as I did, allow it to grow you.

CHAPTER TWENTY-ONE

The Side Chick Epidemic

*Who can find a virtuous woman? For her price is far
above rubies.*

- Proverbs 31:10 (KJV) -

When one thinks of a woman, many different images may
come to mind. These images may consist of a mother, grand-
mother, daughter, sister, aunt, niece, cousin, friend, and/or
wife. A woman's role in life is vital. We are important. This level
of importance is reflected from the very beginning of creation.
After God created Adam, He gave him the task of naming the
animals. Upon Adam completing this task, it became clear
that the animals alone were not suitable or enough for him.
In revealing to Adam how special the woman is, God created
her from apart of Adam himself, his rib (see Genesis 2:18-23).
From the very beginning of time, women were created for a
purpose. Unfortunately, not all women understand this, nor do
we always live up to this standard. As individuals, we struggle
with insecurities, it is inevitable. But insecurities women deal

with can only truly be understood by other women, which is why it's very important for women to support and encourage one another. I have always been an advocate for girl power, and "I am my sister's keeper" has always reigned in my world and heart, which is why I've never taken an interest in another woman's man. Aside from the respect I've shown toward other women, I've also respected myself enough to know I deserve more than being the woman on the side. I've found it difficult to understand why so many women intentionally hurt one another. The lack of respect I received from the women my husband was involved with, is what prompted me to consider why some women resort to this type of behavior. It was revealed to me that hurt people, hurt people. Although this concept is true, it doesn't have to remain a reality. Things can change and hurt people can receive healing and start helping one another. Before beginning to understand the prevalence of side chicks, we must first understand why women are hurt in the first place. There's a reason why women are okay with being the other woman, the mistress, the second choice, the last resort. There's a deep-rooted issue.

Some women would argue they're okay with being the other woman, because they're not looking to be in a relationship or their too busy and focused on other things. What they're really saying is, they don't think they're capable of achieving a meaningful monogamous relationship. Therefore, they convince themselves they aren't relationship material and ultimately, they settle. There's a deep-rooted issue.

Other women's reasoning is since they are getting what they want from the relationship, such as bills being paid, money, gifts, trips, and handbags, then they're fine with being the other woman. What they are saying is: I don't believe I'm capable of attaining the level of success I need to provide myself with the lifestyle I desire, so I'll settle for a man getting those things for me. In this case, material possessions override morals and values, causing them to settle. There's a deep-rooted issue.

Some women also settle for being the side chick because they lack self-confidence, self-esteem, and respect for themselves. They aren't happy with themselves and perhaps wish they had someone else's life. Therefore, the closest way of achieving this is by being the other woman. They convince themselves to believe the wife deserves what she is getting, and her husband wouldn't be cheating if she was fulfilling her wifely duties. Again, this woman settles because there is a deep-rooted issue.

Then, there's the hopeful side chicks. They are loyal to the man, they will keep the affair a secret and if approached, they will deny ever being involved with him. This woman will protect the man and all his lies by any means necessary. In her mind, she has his back. Even though she is aware he has a wife, she isn't involved with anyone else but him. This type of woman stands by in hopes that the loyalty she's shown him will one day pay off and he'll end up leaving his wife to be with her. There's a deep-rooted issue, and the way of getting to the core of these deep-rooted issues is by first looking at one's self.

Look in the mirror, not the outward appearance, but the inner. You may be the most beautiful girl, have the prettiest hair, great style, multiple degrees, and a great career. But when you look deep inside, you discover truth. You realize your insecurities, your flaws, and even your fears have caused you to make choices that have devalued you as a woman. A woman realizing her worth is imperative for her to live a life filled with joy and happiness. If she doesn't understand this, she will always struggle with self-esteem issues. She will always allow herself to be used by men, she will always play second fiddle to another woman, and she will never experience true love. A queen exudes power and is supremely respected. A woman's actions reflect the level of respect she has for herself. What's interesting is that women get upset when men mistreat and disrespect them, but it's okay for them to do it to themselves. Remember this, men love and respect women who love and respect themselves. They know those women who they can manipulate and use. The respect is lost the moment you accept being his side chick. You've accepted that position, and more than likely that's all you will ever be to him. He has no other use or desire for you other than that. In reality, you are just the road he'll cross to get back to his wife.

I say these things not to offend or hurt or anyone, but to encourage you, encourage you to love yourself better. We as Women deserve to be treated like the queens we are. Never settle for a man giving you any less. You deserve for a man to be proud to have you on his arm, instead of denying you and keeping you a secret. You deserve to be taken on dates, and not only spending time together at your home. You deserve better than what you have been accepting and it starts with the person staring back at you in the mirror. It's time to discover and embrace the woman God created. It is then when you will truly begin to live a life of value and great joy.

Women are fearfully and wonderfully made. However, if we fail to tap into that part of us, we fall into the enemy's trap of becoming something contrary to God's plan for our lives. This is right where Satan wants you. He messes with your mind. Before you know it, you start thinking you aren't good enough, pretty enough, smart enough, no man will ever want you, you're too fat, too skinny, and so on and so forth. Satan knows our weaknesses and he uses them against us. Some women may struggle with feelings of unworthiness. Maybe as a child you were never truly loved by a parent, maybe you've had your heart broken, or someone has humiliated you in some way and you've started believing the lies about yourself. The enemy plants these seeds of doubt and before you know it, you start believing it. The devil is God's opponent. He opposes everything good, everything God. His goal is destruction. The trick to defeating him is rebuking everything he tells you. The human mind is extremely powerful, which is why Satan attacks us through our minds. If he's able to get into our mind, he's able to control what we think and ultimately what we do. I encourage you to never listen to Satan, you are of value to God. If you were the only person on earth, God would have still sent His only son to die for you. He created you, and because He created you, you are special. We as women must start showing God that we appreciate Him, and it begins with respecting ourselves, valuing ourselves, uplifting one another, and living up to the standard God placed upon us from the very beginning of creation.

CHAPTER TWENTY-TWO

The Ultimate Test

If you forgive those who sin against you, your heavenly Father will forgive you. But if you refuse to forgive others, your Father will not forgive your sins.

~Matthew 6:14-15~

I was taught early in life that when you do wrong or hurt someone's feelings, you apologize for it. What I've come to learn is that everyone doesn't view it this way. Some people truly have an issue taking accountability for their wrongs. This world is filled with prideful people, and I've learned that regardless if someone apologizes or not, forgiving them has absolutely nothing to do with them, but everything to do with you.

Although my husband had apologized over and over for what he had done, I wasn't open to receiving it. The truth of the matter is, I didn't believe it was sincere. He had done so much, and made the same mistakes over and over, and I just didn't believe him. I was hesitant and skeptical, and forgiving him wasn't something I felt I could ever do. I didn't want to continue to fall for his lies, and because of this, I held a grudge. Although I knew that what I was doing was wrong, I just couldn't find it in me to forgive him. Also, because of the things his family had done, forgiving them was a longshot. Because they didn't have any remorse for the way they treated me, it made it easier for me to hold a grudge. However, it didn't take them apologizing for me to forgive them, it took me deciding to please the Lord instead of my flesh. No matter what a person has done and how you feel, nothing justifies unforgiveness. God forgives us for anything we do, it doesn't matter how big or small it is. He forgives us and commands us to extend the same forgiveness to others. I realized holding on to the hurt and pain was only hindering me, therefore I had to make the decision to let it go.

One reason we resist forgiving, is because we don't understand what it truly means to forgive. We assume that if we forgive those who have wronged us, then this automatically lets them off the hook, and ultimately dismisses our feelings. We believe we are the ones who suffer while those who hurt us go on with their lives as if nothing ever happened. Truth is, we all must answer to God for the wrong we do. It is not our place regarding how and when someone will answer for their wrong, this is God's business.

If you think as I once did, that forgiving someone means you must allow them back into your lives only to give them the opportunity to repeat the same offense, then you're wrong.

While God instructs us to forgive, because it's righteous and sets us free, He doesn't expect for us to continue to trust those who have violated us, or to even be associated with those who have hurt us. Just because you forgive, it doesn't mean you must be reconciled to that person. In no way, shape, or form does God command us to allow those individuals the same access they once had in our lives. You may never be besties, pals, or buddies, and that's okay. In most cases, that is probably the wise thing to do. What I've come to learn is that you should never feel bad for protecting yourself, your space, your energy, and your peace of mind.

I'm sure we all have experienced people saying to us: *let it go, move on,* or *I can't believe you're still tripping off that.* Well, we all deal with things differently and in our own time. Just because someone else may be quick to get over something doesn't mean you will. True forgiveness is a process and doesn't happen overnight. It takes time, and no one should ever be pressured to forgive. If a person isn't genuinely ready to forgive and move forward, being pressured to forgive will only lead to false forgiveness. Before you know it, you'll find yourself right back at square one. If you're like me, a person who has forgiven someone repeatedly, then you may have wondered when is it okay for you to say, "not this time". The book of Matthew 18:21-22 says, Then Peter came to him and asked, "Lord, how often should I forgive someone who sins against me? Seven times?" "No, not seven times," Jesus replied, "but seventy times seven!" There's no limitation on forgiveness. If we find ourselves constantly having to forgive the same person for the same reasons, then we should look at the overall picture. Is it something we are doing that places us in a situation where we are continuing to be hurt, disrespected, attacked, or abused? Not all times are we the cause of things happening to us, but there are times we can prevent certain situations from reoccurring. Using wisdom when involving people and situations can ultimately prevent a person from experiencing unnecessary hurt and pain.

Because God commands us to forgive, we must let go of whatever it is we are holding onto. As I began to understand this from a spiritual standpoint, I realized I had to let go and trust God. Romans 12:19 says, "Dear friends, never take revenge. Leave that to the righteous anger of God." For the Scriptures say, "I will take revenge; I will pay them back," says the Lord. When we refuse to give our situations to God and we seek revenge, we are telling God that we don't trust Him to take care of us. Forgiveness doesn't always appear to be fair, but it is always necessary. No matter how difficult it was, for the sake of my peace of mind and salvation, I chose forgiveness.

Forgiveness begins with maturity. It's a decision that you make because you want to first please God and second no longer be bound to the past. When I made the decision and effort to forgive, healing didn't begin right away. It took both time and effort. It was a process, consisting of emotional ups and downs. One day I was hopeful, and then the next there's a flashback of the past and I'm angry all over again. Although it's normal for memories and emotions to resurface, I couldn't help feeling like there were times I was reliving everything I had gone through. What I hadn't understood is that God was showing me how significant forgiveness is. It's not about our thoughts of the past that matters, it's about what we choose to do with those thoughts. Do we revert to the past, or do we thank God for the strength to move forward? At one point, I didn't think I could move on. I was so stuck in the past, that even the thought of it made me furious. This is when patience stepped in. Because healing is a process, patience is vital. You don't just wake up one day totally healed from a situation, it takes time and a lot of prayer. The path toward rebuilding trust requires a willing spirit. There were times I wanted to give up and say forget it, but because I knew moving forward was best, I remained patient. "I waited patiently for the LORD to help me, and he turned to me and heard my cry," (Psalm 40:1).

I once read in a daily devotional that if someone who has broken the trust of their spouse through betrayal isn't willing to spend the rest of their days earning that trust back without defensiveness, then they lack perspective of what they deserve considering the opportunity they have been given. Although my husband was showing me he didn't want to lose me and was willing to do whatever it took to regain my trust, I didn't believe he was truly up for the challenge. I didn't have any hope in him and couldn't fathom the idea of us working toward rebuilding our marriage. It was difficult for me to get pass the dishonor he brought upon our union. To be intimate with someone other than your wife and say it was a mistake, then to go home to your wife who you went before God and promised to love and honor, was a complete disgrace. Adultery is the most disgusting, selfish, undignified, disrespectful thing a person can do to someone they have vowed to love. Not only does it break the individual, the trust is also broken and almost impossible to reestablish. Although I was broken, I still had to forgive.

It's easy to feel that you've moved passed a situation, gotten over it, and even forgiven when you're not around that individual. But the moment you're reminded of the past is when you realize you haven't in fact moved on. Becoming angry when your past is brought up is a sign that you haven't let it go. I hadn't seen or heard from my husband's parents, but the moment I was reminded of what they had done, old emotions began to resurface. I didn't like being in this place, I didn't want these people and what they had done to have that sort of impact and power over me. I truly wanted to be completely healed from it, but the resentment I had toward them made it challenging. My past was controlling me, my present was greatly affected and eventually my future would be, too, if I didn't do anything about it. This was not the way I envisioned my life. I had the choice to either forgive or continue to be angry. Throughout our lives, people are going to hurt us. We can choose to be mad and allow it to consume us or learn from it and focus on the positive. We must stop expecting anything more from people than what they're capable of giving. Believe them to be who they have shown themselves to be and start responding to them differently. We must stop allowing our past hurts to hinder and control our thoughts, emotions, actions, and lives. While God wants us to be trustworthy people and have people in our lives whom we can trust, He is the only one who can be trusted 100 percent. He will never fail us. But we must learn to understand and accept that man will, and it's simply because we are not perfect. "For all have sinned and fall short of the glory of God," (Romans 3:23, NIV). At some point in our lives and regardless of how extreme it may be, we all have been the cause of another person's pain. Some people may acknowledge their wrongs and learn from them while others don't. Either way, this isn't our concern; it's between them and God. God extends grace to us daily and therefore we should do the same for others. My personal experiences helped me to understand that anger is a feeling and how we respond to it is a choice. When you decide that you will respond to others with the same grace, love, and forgiveness that God offers you, that's when you have come to understand the true meaning of forgiveness. All the wrong that was done to me has no bearing on the magnitude of God's love and kindness toward me. Because God values me and because of my desire to please Him, I have chosen to be obedient to His word. I have chosen to forgive.

CHAPTER TWENTY-THREE

Seasons Change

*To everything there is a season, and a time to every
purpose under the heaven.*

~Ecclesiastes 3:1 KJV~

Change. How would someone define this six-letter word?
If you were to ask a group of people this question, I'm almost
positive just about everyone would have similar responses.
Although this word means something becoming different,
it's not as simplistic as it sounds. Change for some people
may be simple, but complicated for others. I believe ones'
own perception of change is based upon their personal experiences. Change affects people in many ways. Some people
handle it well, while others not so well. Nonetheless, change
is unavoidable. It's something we have no control over; it
happens whether we want it to or not. Some change is good
and some not so good, but there's always a lesson in it.

Throughout my life, I've encountered many changes.
Whether it was leaving home and going off to college, my

parents divorcing, losing a loved one, getting married, starting a new career, or giving birth to my daughter, I learned that embracing change makes the transition smoother than it does resisting it. Change is there to develop us, it serves as a portal for reaching our destination: our destiny. There has always been some sort of lesson within any trial I've encountered. I didn't always immediately realize what that lesson was, but over time, it was revealed. God sometimes uses our circumstances as a way of removing certain things or people from our lives. During the toughest storm of my life, and just when I thought things couldn't get any worse, they did. As my circumstances changed, friendships also began to change. It's in our toughest of times when we discover who's truly in our corner. We've all heard the saying, "when it rains it pours." Well, I'm a living testament of this. For example, when a storm occurs, there's disarray, and the aftermath of that storm tends to be unbearable. But once the storm has passed, the sun begins to shine. When this happened for me, my perspective on life was different. God allows storms in our lives as a way of altering things. In hindsight, God was wanting more from me and He knew the only way to get my full attention was by rearranging certain areas in my life, and one of those areas was friendship.

Friendship is important and a vital part of life. It's also a two-way street that consists of different levels. Nonetheless, if I call you my friend, it means I hold you at high regard and expect the same in return. I'm a loyal person, but what I've learned is that everyone isn't going to be the same type of friend you are. Realistically, we all are different with different views, intentions, and values. Is this a bad thing? Well, that depends on how you view it. With any relationship, no one should stand by and allow someone to give them less than what they deserve. There should always be standards and expectations. Is everything going to be good all the time? Absolutely not. There are going to be ups and downs, but it's important to discern whether the friendship is experiencing a hiccup or a hindrance. Is the friendship challenging you? Is it of substance? Is it helping you to grow and become a better person? Are you learning from it? When you leave from the person's presence do you feel uplifted and empowered or do you feel drained? These are all important factors to consider. Sometimes, it's as simple as two people outgrowing one another.

I like to use the phrase, "growing pains" to describe what sometimes takes place within friendships. I remember as a child I would get this horrible pain in my legs. After my mother had taken me to the doctor, we learned it was growing pains. It's been said that growing pains occur when a child is going through a growth spurt. As adults, we may be done growing physically, but this doesn't mean we aren't growing spiritually, mentally, and emotionally. It can be painful, because as you outgrow some relationships, you find yourself having to adjust to a new life. This process wasn't easy for me, but I knew it was necessary. Some friendships I believed would have lasted a lifetime either shifted or dissolved. Even those that lasted as long as twenty plus years had reached their expiration date. To sum it up, not everyone you start out with, you're going to finish with. People are placed in our lives for a purpose and we must begin using wisdom in knowing when their purpose has been fulfilled. So here I am, dealing with my husband's infidelity, our marriage publicized, feeling judged and humiliated, being harassed, and now of all times, God decides to reveal my true friends. All I could think was, why me and why did He choose this moment? Truth is, God makes no mistakes and His timing is always perfect. Whatever He was doing, I trusted it was for my good.

There isn't anyone in this world who doesn't need a friend. Scripture tells us, "For if they fall, one will lift up his fellow. But woe to him who is alone when he falls and has not another to lift him up," (Ecclesiastes 4:10, KJV). We all need someone. This is God's purpose for friendship. God never intended for us to face trials on our own, therefore he's given us the gift of friendship. However, not everyone values it. Friends ought to share in great times with one another, as well as being there in those times that are not so great. Something is wrong when a friend is only there in the good times, in the happy times, when it's easy, but nowhere to be found when the going gets tough. Is this really a friendship? When someone is dealing with a life altering situation, having support is vital. Some friends didn't support me the way I would have expected them to. They either judged, gossiped, or expressed how they felt I was wrong. I understand as individuals we are entitled to our opinion and I'm totally okay with this. However, I believe it's possible to have an opinion while also being there for your friend in their time of need. When this didn't happen, I realized those friends I once held to a high standard and believed cherished my friendship with them as well, turned out to be different. I had already hit rock bottom and the last thing I needed was to feel like I was being kicked when I was already down. Nevertheless, I trusted the process knowing there was a much greater purpose behind it.

Even though certain friendships ended, it doesn't negate the fact these were once people I grew up with, was close with, shared secrets with, and truly cared for. Therefore, I will always have love for them. Each friendship served its purpose, and I am grateful for the lessons they taught me. However, through this experience, God revealed my true friends. As much as I love and cherish family, God also revealed those family members who were truly in my corner. I am grateful for my family and friends, they were there helping me to weather the most devastating storm of my life. They never left my side, they didn't tell me what I wanted to hear, but what I needed to hear. They prayed for me when I wasn't strong enough to pray for myself, they checked up on me, they visited with me, they didn't judge or attempt to make me feel worse than I had already felt, they had my back. They didn't give up on me when times were tough; they were there, encouraging me and helping me to get through it. God specifically placed them in my life and because of them, I know real friends do exist.

When God has an assignment on your life, some things must change. Had it not been for what I had gone through publicly, I would probably still be holding on to certain relationships. So often we find ourselves holding on even when God is telling us to let go. When we enter a new season, it sometimes consists of us leaving the old stuff behind: the stuff that's no longer working, no longer good, no longer right, and no longer meant to be a part of our lives. I've found the process that takes place when the Fall season ends, and Spring begins to be interesting in the aspect that it's relative to what sometimes takes place within relationships. The term deciduous means "falling off at maturity." This occurs when trees shed their leaves in the Fall season. After leaves fall off and the Spring season approaches, new leaves begin to sprout. Falling off at maturity is essential for new leaves to grow, just as shedding outgrown relationships is essential for individual growth. The sprouting of the leaves in the Spring is symbolic of evolving. We must stop wasting time on lifeless situations, relationships, and people. If it's dead, it's dead for a reason. People will come, and people will go. Life is constantly changing, and nothing ever stays the same. Even when life becomes overwhelming with just about every aspect changing, God promises one thing that will never change, and that's Himself. His word will endure the test of time and we can trust and find stability in it. Through this experience, I've learned no matter how people, relationships, circumstances, and the world changes, God will always remain the same.

CHAPTER TWENTY-FOUR

It's Necessary

> *"For I know the plans I have for you," says the LORD. "They are plans for good and not for disaster, to give you a future and a hope."*
>
> *~Jeremiah 29:11~*

When there's an anointing on your life, tribulations will follow. I always wondered why God allowed me to experience certain trials. Come to find out those trials were designed to test, develop, and prepare me for my destiny. "To whom much is given much is required," (Luke 12:48). There are times we want the benefit without having to do the work. We want everything easy and resist the tough times. However, we must recognize that when life is uncomfortable, God is doing His best work in us.

Sometimes, it takes a crisis to see Christ. I am a total believer that had I not made that phone call, my marriage wouldn't even be where it is. Through this trial, God shifted some things within my life, and I am grateful for it. When the incident first occurred, I felt an extreme amount of regret and guilt. Since then, that has changed. I now know the issues I encountered with my husband's family, his infidelity, the way it was revealed, the phone call, and even the public embarrassment was all a part of God's perfect plan. It needed to happen this way and more importantly, God allowed it to happen this way. It was for a greater purpose. That call was a vital piece of the puzzle. Even though it was painful and humiliating, I embrace it. It has made me stronger and has strengthened my marriage in the process. Right before my eyes, God began to deliver and change my husband. The challenges my marriage faced were placed there to strengthen it and draw my husband and myself closer to God. Had it not occurred, neither of us would be where we are spiritually. God opened my husband's eyes and allowed him to see things clearly. His way of thinking became different, the way he spoke was different, and even the way he acted was different. None of this would have been possible without the sovereign power of God. Fighting tooth and nail, marriage counseling, and even separating, wasn't enough to change my husband. It took us going through something drastic, something devastating, and something detrimental for a change to occur. Sometimes, God allows something terrible to happen as a way of grasping our attention. God permitted my marriage to reach the level of destruction it did for Him to restore it and for my husband to be delivered.

As I began to see a change in my husband, I was amazed. After all the back and forth and ups and downs, never in a million years did I think it would happen. At one point, I started believing there was no hope for him. I felt the bondage he was attached to was too deep and him changing was impossible. Then I was reminded of the story of Sarah. God told Sarah at 90 years old she would give birth to a child. Sarah laughed at God and didn't believe it (see Genesis 18:1 – 18:15). I relate to this story, because as much as I wanted to give up on my marriage, God wouldn't let me. He kept telling me to be patient and in time things would get better. However, just like Sarah, I didn't believe it was possible. Nevertheless, God responded just as He responded to Sarah's situation saying, "Is anything too hard for me?" When you truly have faith in God, the type of faith that is unwavering, you believe and trust that with Him all things are possible, even when they seem impossible. All along I had been viewing my situation from a natural lens instead of a spiritual one. Doing this caused me to miss the message God was revealing to me. We are imperfect people, and therefore we sometimes doubt and even forget that there is absolutely nothing God cannot do. Scripture tells us, "It was by faith that even Sarah was able to have a child, though she was barren and was too old. She believed that God would keep his promise," (Hebrews 11:11). God has proven over and over to do just as He said He would. Through experience I've come to know, there's nothing too big for God. He's done the impossible for me and He will do it for you.

Paul stated in the book of Galatians 2:20; "My old self has been crucified with Christ. It is no longer I who live, but

Christ lives in me." What he meant by this is that his old self, his old ways and beliefs, have died. Paul no longer found life in the things of the world, in fact he was glad to be living a Christ-filled life. Paul even expressed, he lives his life by faith in Jesus, believing that Jesus knows what's best for his life, because He loves him and gave up His life for him (see Galatians 2:20). This is what happens when someone completely surrenders their life to God. They become free from all the things of their past life, and in turn, they begin living for God. To surrender means to give up control and to deny self and relinquish things like needing to be in charge or needing to have all the answers in advance. It means walking with God, even in the unknown, and trusting Him to lead and provide. Surrendering is realizing your life is not your own, that it solely belongs to God.

It was when a visible change began to take place within my husband that I knew it was God. There were quite a few things in which God began to deliver my husband from, and a major one was dishonesty. My husband struggled with being honest. In fact, most of the problems we faced were because of his dishonesty. This was his reputation. When the word integrity is broken down, it brings great understanding to its meaning. Integrity is associated with the word integer. An integer is a whole number, not a fraction or decimal. An integer is complete. To have integrity is to be the same through and through, front to back, all around, in private and public, inside and outside, it is to be complete with morals and values. The consistency between our inner disposition and our outward behavior reflects one another when we possess integrity. Even if the two don't mirror one another, God has the power to move in our lives to shape our integrity. Where my husband once lacked integrity, God stepped in and established it. I couldn't help but wonder why God hadn't done this for my husband a long time ago. I'm sure it would have prevented a lot of what we experienced in our marriage from occurring. The truth is, God doesn't always move when we want Him to. He operates on and in His own time. God knew back then that my husband wasn't in a place where he was willing to receive change; he didn't feel he needed to change. Therefore, it took God placing him in a position where he had no other choice but to surrender to Him.

Another area in which God transformed my husband was in obedience. Obedience is one of the first qualities God forms within us. It may not always be as easy as we would like it to be, but He gives us the strength we need once we make the choice to obey. Obedience is one of the ways we demonstrate our love for God. The Bible tells us, "So you must live as God's obedient children. Don't slip back into your old ways of living to satisfy your own desires. You didn't know any better then" (Peter 1:14). A true change warrants true obedience. I would always say to my husband, "if you live according to the will of God, most of the problems we face wouldn't exist." When a married person is truly saved, their desire would normally be for their spouse to be as well. This makes the marriage easier because you both are on the same page in that you're living to please the Lord. I knew it would take for my husband surrendering to God for us to be completely happy in our marriage. Even though I wanted my husband to change, I made it clear that I didn't want him changing for me. I believe that changing for a person other than yourself would only be temporary, but a true change is when a person wants to change and allows themselves to be changed by God.

I recall overhearing my husband telling someone if it wasn't for me, he wouldn't have a relationship with God. When I told him that I heard what he said, he began to tell me that prior to meeting me, he didn't know much about God. He thanked me and told me how much he appreciated me. My husband would have never admitted this before, and although I had already heard him saying this to someone else, it meant so much more coming from him. This reflected humility and vulnerability. I truly believe God sometimes uses certain people to draw others closer to Him. I now believe one of the main reasons God placed my husband and I together was for me to be the Godly example he needed. 1 Peter 3:1 says, "In the same way, you wives must accept the authority of your husbands. Then, even if some refuse to obey the Good News, your Godly lives will speak to them without any words. They will be won over by observing your pure and reverent lives." God saved my husband through me. As wives, we were created to be help meets. God said in Genesis 2:18, "It is not good for the man to be alone. I will make a helper who is just right for him." In examining the meaning of "help meet," I've discovered it to be more than a helper or companion. For instance, in Hebrew there are two words that "help meet" is derived from, "ezer," and 'k'enegdo." The word ezer consists of two roots: one meaning "to rescue, to save," and the other meaning "to be strong." The word kenegdo means, "in front of" or "opposite." Eve was not designed to be exactly like Adam. She was designed to be his mirror opposite, possessing the other half of the qualities and attributes in which he lacked. Women are "helpers" to men in that they nurture them toward Christ. In reflecting on this, I began to realize that when men and women truly understand they have been blessed with different responsibilities, gifts, and abilities, they can then begin to work together as one. Husbands and wives need each other, but more importantly, we need God.

I've learned more in the past year than I have in my entire life. Very early in our marriage, my former pastor said the following statement to my husband and I, "Satan wants your marriage." I couldn't have agreed more with him. Satan spends most of his time trying to cause division. His attack is on marriage because he knows that God's power and glory are both achieved and magnified through unity. Jesus knew their thoughts and said to them, "Every kingdom divided against itself will be ruined, and every city or household divided against itself will not stand" (Matthew 12:25, NIV). To truly stand means we must stand together as one. My house wasn't standing because we both opened the door for the enemy to come in. I was focused on my husband's wrongs and he was focused on diverting from them. This resulted in us both neglecting to see what Satan was doing. Nonetheless, God covered us. His favor didn't cease because we both were too blind and distracted by our own desires. My prayer was for God to align our hearts, minds and spirits. I also prayed He would help us to view our marriage as more than just a relationship that would bring each of us pleasure or satisfy our own personal needs, but to please Him instead. When we choose to view marriage through God's eyes, it helps us to live according to His will. For my husband and I to grow and be united on a deeper level, it took us fully understanding God's purpose for our marriage. When married couples function together in being of the same mind, maintaining the same love, united in spirit, and intent of God's purpose, it is then that God's will for marriage is fulfilled. The word of God says, "So then let us pursue what makes for peace and for mutual upbuilding," (Romans 14:19). Husbands and wives are to seek, say, and do things that build each other up in Christ. This was the mindset we both had to adopt for God to move in our marriage and toward complete restoration.

God will get our attention one way or another. He gives us opportunities on top of opportunities and when we don't surrender and move, He does. God has shown how powerful He is in that something that was meant to destroy us, He allowed it to work for our good. I'm a testament that regardless of the state your life is in right now, God is always in control. There was a purpose for everything that occurred in my marriage. I remember a while back God telling me that there would be a change in my husband's career. Years later, my husband came to me and said he needed to talk with me about something. As curiosity grew, he told me he had been thinking of retiring from politics and wanted to know my thoughts. My advice was for him to pray about it and trust that God will direct him in making the right decision. I was completely shocked. My husband wanted to know my opinion, he cared what I thought, and even consulted with me before making a decision. This was our breakthrough moment. I couldn't do anything but praise God. Everything He had told me, was coming to pass. I had never asked my husband to walk away from his job. He didn't see how his job negatively affected him and our marriage. He didn't even see how he once loved politics so much that he put it before everything. It literally took God opening my husband's eyes to see things clearly, to see things the way God sees them. God has proven that He is able to do exceedingly, abundantly, above all we can ask or think. I didn't give up on my husband, I didn't give up on my marriage, I listened to God and hung in there; and in the end, my husband received his deliverance.

It was all necessary; the infidelity, the phone call, and even the public humiliation. Who knew I would endure the most difficult trial of my life as a way for my husband to be saved. God knew it, it was His plan all along. Redemptive suffering is when you go through a problem or pain for the benefit of someone else. All the hurt, pain, suffering, and going through hell was worth it because my husband's life was saved. I'm grateful my marriage went through its low points, because had it not, we wouldn't appreciate the highs. Nothing that happens in our lives is in vain, there's a purpose for everything. You may be going through something right now, but I encourage you to hold on and don't give up. Even in those times when God seems to be silent, He's working behind the scenes on your behalf. No matter how tough it gets, how devastating it is, or how impossible it may appear, in the end, it's necessary.

CHAPTER TWENTY-FIVE

Refined

> *But he knoweth the way that I take; when he hath tried me, I shall come forth as gold.*
>
> *~Job 23:10 KJV~*

Gold goes through a process of purification, and just like gold, we as people go through the same process. Gold is made by fire and we are made by our trials. When God takes us through, it isn't to cause us harm, it's for our good. The above scripture says, after being tried, you come out as pure gold. To be classified as gold, means you are personally approved and improved by God. You've been tested, you've endured, and you have overcome.

What God was doing within me was life changing. In Him dealing with me, I began spending more time with Him, reading His word, and praying more. The more I grew spiritually, the better I understood the significance behind all I had endured. God was working on the inside of me and completely rearranging my life. It first started with Him removing those things from my life that was preventing me from growing, causing me unhappiness, and ultimately hindering me from completely living a life pleasing to Him. We don't always realize the amount of baggage we hold onto and how it has the capability of hindering our spiritual growth. As God began removing certain people and situations from my life, He also began to show me why. Where He was taking me, everyone wasn't going to understand. Therefore, there couldn't be any distractions. It was just me and Him. He was transforming me. My faith was being established, I was being refined. There were times I wanted to give up and felt I wouldn't make it through, but in the word of God, I found hope. 1 Peter 1:7 says, "These trials will show that your faith is genuine. It is being tested as fire tests and purifies gold—though your faith is far more precious than mere gold. So, when your faith remains strong through many trials, it will bring you much praise and glory and honor on the day when Jesus Christ is revealed to the whole world." The process is intense because of the pressure that's being applied in removing things within us that are not supposed to be there. Although I questioned God many times, I learned the very thing I believed to be destroying me. Turned out, God was using it to bless me.

When God takes us through the fire, His intent is always to bring us out better. The last thing most people want to hear is they need to change. Even the idea of change can bring about resistance. We often find ourselves in a state of contentment and feel there isn't a reason for us to change. However, for us to become who God intends us to be, we must go through the process. The last year of my life has been chaotic. Although I was tried in ways I never imagined, it was all a part of my spiritual makeover. This has been quite a journey, consisting of countless lessons along the way. One of those lessons is that having a relationship with God gives us strength to face anything. I also learned the harder you fall, the higher you will bounce back up. Will there be scratches and bruises? Yes, but in the end, there's always healing. God is always there, willing to move in your life if you allow Him. He teaches us, shapes us, builds our character, instills virtues in us, and forms values within us, all while helping us to discover who we are in Him.

Although my life hasn't always been easy, I wouldn't change it for anything. I love me, and I love the person I've become. Amongst many attributes, I am a woman who limitlessly loves the Lord, stands up for what's right, and isn't afraid to boldly declare the goodness of God. My life has consisted of an array of ups and downs, twists and turns; but through it all, I didn't give up. Because of this, I'm able to be a witness to others about what God can do when you completely trust in Him. Because of God, I'm at peace and my heart is filled with joy. I've been blessed with a new life; I'm revived, I'm renewed, and I am refined.

CHAPTER TWENTY-SIX

Love Wins

*Love is patient, love is kind. It does not envy, it
does not boast, it is not proud. It does not dishonor
others, it is not self-seeking, it is not easily angered,
it keeps no record of wrongs. Love does not delight
in evil but rejoices with the truth. It always protects,
always trusts, always hopes, always perseveres. Love
never fails.*

~ 1 Corinthians 13:4-8 ~

I've heard the saying, "The truth can either hurt you or change you." Well, in my case, it did both. In life, we experience different levels of hurt and pain, but we can count them all as learning experiences. Never in a million years did I imagine facing an indescribable degree of pain and humiliation from someone I vowed to love for the rest of my life. As I was experiencing turmoil within my own marriage, God began to reveal so many others were as well. So often we feel ashamed and alone as though no one can relate or understand what we are going through, not knowing so many others are going through some of the same exact things.

There's a thing called female liberation. As women we are strong, we stand up for ourselves, and would never stand for being cheated on, walked over, or taken for granted. The first time a man does something wrong, we are done. There isn't any explaining, pleading, nor second chances, it's simply over. But that's until it actually happens. Reality kicks in and we find ourselves in situations where we've been cheated on, misused, and so on and so forth. Suddenly, that same female liberation talk we once stood so strongly for is thrown out of the window. So much for being liberated, right? Truth is, you never know how you will react to something until experiencing it for yourself. Although we as women should never condone being treated like anything less than a queen, we must understand there's a false reality regarding the term: female liberation. This mindset doesn't embrace the human component. It doesn't take into consideration that because we are human, we are imperfect and are likely to make mistakes. What's important is making the right choice for you. It's also important for this to be done without the interference and opinion of others. This is exactly what I had to do. If you decide to stay, as I did, some people may call it being stupid, which is totally fine. Nonetheless, life has taught me that I cannot be concerned with the opinions of others, especially those who don't have my best interest at heart. Although I used the word "stay", I must say in no way was I willing to "stay" in the same mess or even under the same circumstances. Had there not been a visible change within my husband, then this part of my story would be totally different.

While so many people were focused on my husband's indiscretions, I was no longer in that place. I decided to push past the pain to make room for love, and my love for God did not allow me to give up on my husband. Although there were times I wanted to, I continued to love him despite his mistakes. This is the type of love God gives us and wants us to give to others. God's love helped me in being open in giving my marriage another chance and an opportunity for growth. I had been married shy of three years, and therefore I felt our marriage hadn't truly developed. There are couples who have been married for decades and who have experienced some things that would blow the minds of a lot of people, yet they didn't give up. In today's world, couples are quick to divorce without the thought of giving their marriage a fighting chance. We've become accustomed to if the marriage doesn't work, divorce is always an option. Wherein back in the day, married couples didn't look to divorce as an option, they made it work. Marriages are sure to encounter good times just as well as bad times. For me, it was horrific times. Nonetheless, if I had chosen to give up, to throw in the towel and divorce, I would have never known if our union was strong enough to withstand the storm. Contrary to what others might have done if they were in my shoes, I made the best choice for me. I chose to fight for a God designed covenant. As a married woman, but also a woman of God, I had to look at the bigger picture. Not only had I made a vow to my husband, I also made a vow to God. Although I had grounds for divorce, I knew divorce wasn't necessarily pleasing to God. It was important for me to fight for what God joined together; I owed it to myself. I also owed my daughter the opportunity to experience a positive example of marriage and a solid foundation of family. As crazy as it may sound, despite the choices my husband made, I even owed it to him. Reason being is that I vowed to be with him for better and for worse; I just didn't know we would have been experiencing the worse so soon. But most importantly, I owed it to God. Marriage is a sacred covenant, not a social contract; therefore, I didn't want to disappoint Him by giving up so easily. God honors marriage, and I trust He will show favor in me choosing to fight for mine.

In today's world, marriage is at the bottom of the priority list, it isn't honored nor valued. People place status, money, career, and other relationships above it. This is exactly how Satan wants us to view marriage. Being aware of this helped me to view things differently. When I once focused on *what* my husband had done, it began to shift to *why*. What I realized is that Satan had a plan from the very beginning. I recall receiving several prophecies that God was going to use my husband and I to do great things together. Well, amidst the storm of my life, this was the last thing on my mind. All I could think of is how terrible things were. However, I eventually began to understand and accept the reason behind my marriage being attacked. Satan was aware of the plans God had for us and therefore, he did everything in his power to block it. Because of God having His hands on our marriage, there was absolutely nothing at all Satan could do to destroy it.

Not only was it God's plan to save and deliver my husband, I realized God was transforming me as well. My view and reaction to certain things changed. I never imagined I would be able to forgive my husband and give our marriage another chance, but I've come to realize marriage doesn't always consist of happiness; a successful marriage consists of forgiveness and promises to never give up. I've learned so much in this period of time than I ever thought was possible. I'm no longer ashamed of the obstacles my marriage faced, without them we wouldn't be where we are today. Because of it, I have learned who I am, who my husband is, and more importantly, who God is. God has given us a new beginning, a chance at love the way He intended. My husband is my best friend, I can honestly say I like him; I mean I truly like him as a person. I am excited about our future and where God is taking us. I am already amazed at how God has turned things around, and I can only imagine what else He has in store for us. Marriage isn't easy at all, but it's a blessing when two people truly love one another and are willing to do whatever it takes to make it work. Despite all the things that caused our marriage harm, in the end, one thing that never changed is the love we have for one another. Love truly conquers all. No matter how people talked about us and said we wouldn't make it, and even with all the odds against us, what God joined together no man could separate. There are two things I've come to learn about love: it's far from perfect and it will always win.

CHAPTER TWENTY-SEVEN

Better Days

And after you have suffered a little while, the God of all grace, who has called you to His eternal glory in Christ, will Himself restore, confirm, strengthen, and establish you.

~1 Peter 5:10 ESV~

Life is a journey and is not intended to be experienced alone. 2016 was the worst year of my life; it was emotional, drama-filled, painful, traumatic, disturbing, hostile, depressing, miserable, discouraging, and broken among so many other things. As horrible as it was, it was also a blessing. God allows us to experience the worst of times to bring us closer to Him. Whatever you've endured throughout your life, turn to God; he can work it out.

If God showed us a snapshot of all the events that would occur in our lives, I'm almost positive we would panic and more than likely begin bargaining with Him to alter the path ahead of us. By no means would we ever think we could survive such difficult circumstances: death of a loved one, lack of parental relationships, or infidelity by a spouse to name a few. It's more than our finite minds can even begin to understand. Because of this, God doesn't show us. Instead, He gives us the strength we need to get through it. I found myself turning to man for help, but nothing changed. That was because I was looking to the wrong source. It is not found in a human being, it's found in the One True Living God. Truth is, people can't do what God can. They may be able to give you advice, some good and some not so good. However, if that advice isn't from God, your situation can turn out being worse than what it was to begin with. Scripture says in Galatians 1:10 NIV, "Am I now trying to win the approval of human beings, or of God? Or am I trying to please people? If I were still trying to please people, I would not be a servant of Christ." I've learned that seeking the will of God will take you much further than seeking the approval of man.

Life has the ability of instantly changing. One day, my life was fine, and then the next, it's turned upside down. Nothing was the same and everything was different. It was the beginning of God altering my life for the better. But before it gets better, we sometimes must first experience the worst. I've been cheated on, I've been talked about, I've been lied on, I've been betrayed, I've been judged, and people have even turned their backs on me; but I'm here today standing stronger than ever. God gives the hardest battles to His strongest soldiers, for it's not how you start, but how you finish. Life's experiences are there to grow us and help us to reach our true purpose in life. I learned the only way for this to take place is by completely surrendering to God. He requires our best; He wants all of us. The moment I stopped trying to control my circumstances and gave it to God, is when He began to truly move in my life. Since then, life has been better and not bitter. Life has been peaceful and not chaotic. Life has been happy and not sad. My healing and restoration began as soon as I decided to surrender to God. I am not saying there won't be tough times, but those tough times won't seem so tough because your outlook will be different. Because I am different, I see things differently and even respond differently. In the past, I would easily fall for the enemy's tricks, but now I'm spiritually grounded and prepared for anything he throws my way. I have been through some stuff, enough to know it's best to rejoice in my trials and not to be overcome by them.

God is taking me higher, I'm closer to my destiny and growing more and more every day. I learned that when the enemy's attacks are frequent, it's because God is elevating you. Satan's plan all along was to break and destroy me, but God's plan to save and restore me was greater. God covers us even in times we don't realize it. Because of my experiences, I am stronger, wiser, and better. I rejoice at the sight of the traps set by the enemy, because I know when it's over, I'm coming-out victorious. Had I not gone through what I did, I wouldn't be the woman I am today. I wouldn't be walking in my purpose. I embrace it all: the good, the bad, and even the ugly, and I am ready for the next chapter of my life.

To every end there is a beginning, and I am looking forward to mine. We've all heard the saying, "When life gives you lemons, make lemonade." However, what do you do when you're unable to make lemonade? You realize you never made your own lemonade to begin with. Your strength comes only from the Lord and He's the source of everything you need. We are not in control of our destiny, God is, and He didn't create us to deal with life's circumstances alone. He's always there guiding us, leading us, and shielding us through it all. As long as we have Him, we can conquer anything. I am a living testament that even through struggles, heartache, sorrow, and disappointment, there's always light at the end of the tunnel. Because of God and God alone, I am here today, living my best days.

About the Author

Latosha Rachelle Carter is a true woman of God with an undeniable anointing over her life. A native of St. Louis, Missouri, Latosha has devoted a vast amount of her life toward helping others. Her infinite passion of being a light to those in need is what led her to pursue a career in the field of social work. Earning a Master of Social Work from Southern Illinois University, Edwardsville, Latosha has experience working with various populations such as: children and families, at risk youth, the homeless community, persons living with HIV/Aids, individuals with mental health illness and the list goes on. She is currently a school social worker serving the St. Louis Metropolitan Area where she takes great pride in leading and guiding students socially, emotionally, and academically. Her bold, yet compassionate and transparent personality is what allows her the capability of effortlessly building rapport with others. She totally has a heart for people. She is relatable and possesses great insight, and without hesitation many are drawn to her. Latosha is a proud member of Delta Sigma Theta Sorority Incorporated and business owner, however it doesn't get in the way of her dedicating her time and service to the Kingdom of God. She serves in her home church in various capacities such as Minister, Deaconess, Member of the Praise Team, Step Ministry Leader and Director of Vacation Bible

School. This dynamic woman is an encourager, inspirer and motivator to many. In her past time, she enjoys reading, traveling, and spending time with loved ones. A woman of many hats, she is indeed, but a loving wife, mother and daughter is what brings her great joy.

Made in the USA
Middletown, DE
05 March 2019